Economics of
Approval Plans

Economics of
Approval Plans

_Proceedings of the Third International Seminar on
Approval and Gathering Plans in Large and
Medium Size Academic Libraries, Held in the Ramada Inn,
West Palm Beach, Florida,
February 17-19, 1971_

PETER SPYERS-DURAN AND DANIEL GORE
Editors

Greenwood Press, Inc., Westport, Connecticut

Library of Congress Cataloging in Publication Data

International Seminar on Approval and Gathering Plans in
    Large and Medium Size Academic Libraries, 3d, West
    Palm Beach, Fla., 1971.
    Economics of approval plans.
    Includes bibliographical references.
        1. Book buying (Libraries)—Congresses. 2. Lib-
raries, University and college. I. Spyers-Duran, Peter,
ed. II. Gore, Daniel, ed. III. Title.
Z689.I54 1971   025.2   72-836
ISBN 0-8371-6405-2

Library of Congress Catalog Card Number: 72-836
ISBN: 0-8371-6405-2
First published in 1972

Greenwood Press, Inc.
Publishing Division
51 Riverside Avenue, Westport, Connecticut 06880

Printed in the United States of America

Contents

Preface

Current budget strains on college and university libraries require a stepped-up search for operating economies. The timely topic of economics of approval plans of the Third International Conference on Approval and Gathering Plans for Large and Medium Size Academic Libraries, held at the Ramada Inn, West Palm Beach, Florida, February 17-19, 1971, has thus generated considerable interest.

The papers published here constitute, by and large, original research in this area. The importance of these contributions can hardly be overestimated, since they will no doubt mold and influence collection development practices in the current imprint area.

David O. Lane searches in his paper for an answer to the question of the effects approval plans have on the nation's academic libraries. While he concludes that approval plans will continue to be somewhat controversial as a collection development tool, the practice is here to stay and is gaining momentum.

Mark Gormley's paper suggests that approval plans can fail

in libraries if the conditions of the plan are not carefully administered and monitored. He places particular emphasis on the need for a good collection development profile and effective, open communications between the jobber and the library.

Bill Axford meticulously depicts actual savings in a state university system using approval plans rather than the traditional item-by-item method of purchasing current imprints.

As the audience expected, Daniel Gore delivered a unique paper full of practical suggestions. His paper contradicts the popular conception that approval plans are only for the wealthier institutions. As the Macalester College experience illustrates, approval plans can be adapted to the modest book budgets of liberal arts colleges.

LeMoyne Anderson and Harriet Rebuldela do an excellent job reviewing efficient systems that libraries could employ to increase the economies that approval plans offer. The summary statement by Richard Chapin is sharp, witty, and analytical. We are most grateful for Dick's performance, crediting him with one of the most difficult tasks of "bringing it all together" at the close of the conference.

The proceedings of the First and Second International Conferences on Approval Plans carry detailed descriptions of the variety of approval plans offered by jobbers here and abroad. Rather than repeat this information, we refer the reader to the appropriate volumes.[1]

The dealers' panel discussion, chaired by Hugh Atkinson, brings out some fine details of improvements, as well as the

---

1. Peter Spyers-Duran, ed., *Approval and Gathering Plans in Academic Libraries* (Littleton, Col.: Libraries Unlimited, Inc., 1969); Peter Spyers-Duran and Daniel Gore, eds., *Advances in Understanding Approval and Gathering Plans in Academic Libraries* (Kalamazoo: Western Michigan University, 1970).

future plans and hopes of leading book experts. This portion of the text will help the reader keep abreast of current developments.

In attendance at the seminar were 103 persons, representing universities and colleges in 31 states, Canada, Germany, France, and England. It was rewarding to note that there were several participants who also attended the first and second conferences in 1968 and 1969, held at Western Michigan University. Seventeen jobbers were represented at this meeting, while just two years ago, only five dealers had enough interest in approval plans to attend the first conference.

We are indebted to the speakers for the preparation and delivery of their papers. These people were chosen because of their knowledge and skill in collection development and, particularly, in approval plans. We are also indebted to the members of the panel and its moderator, Hugh Atkinson, for their willingness to share their experiences and knowledge with us.

I am personally grateful to the Florida Atlantic University Library staff for their assistance in every detail of the conference. The conference ran smoothly throughout because of their dedication to the success of that operation.

The conference chairman also wishes to express his appreciation to Dan Gore, co-editor of the proceedings.

Cordial thanks are extended to the Richard Abel Company, The Baker & Taylor Company, Blackwell's, Bro-Dart Industries, Alexander Broude, Inc., and Otto Harrassowitz for supporting the hospitality arrangements enjoyed by the entire group.

Special thanks are due to Mr. Robert Kizlik, representing FAU's Division of Continuing Education, for his aid in the conference arrangements and to Mr. Eugene A. Robinson, Special Assistant to the President, FAU, for his welcoming address.

Peter Spyers-Duran

Economics of
Approval Plans

1

Economics of
Approval Plans

H. William Axford

Looking back over the past two decades, one can see that three major issues seem to have dominated discussions among academic librarians: (1) the relative merits of the Library of Congress classification system compared to Dewey decimal; (2) the role of the computer in library operations; and (3) blanket-approval plans as a means for systematic collection development. All three have generated considerable amounts of impassioned rhetoric at professional gatherings, a corpus of polemical writing, but only a relatively small amount of research aimed at evaluating how the Library of Congress classification system, the computer, or approval plans have advanced or retarded the academic library's progress toward its stated educational objectives. Nevertheless, the trend toward the Library of Congress classification system continues to accelerate, the use and abuse of the computer is increasingly evident, and the number of academic libraries utilizing approval plans grows with each passing year, as does the number of firms offering them.

This situation suggests at least two possibilities: academic librarians may be inclined to rush into anything that carries the magic connotation of being innovative or experimental or there is something inherently rational about all three of these developments—that they are related to a slowly evolving network for the acquisition, bibliographic control, and dissemination of knowledge on a global scale, which overarches the individual libraries that are its constituent parts. In all probability, both possibilities have been operative. But, I would prefer to believe that the latter has been by far the most important—that these trends reflect the intuitive genius and pragmatically oriented intellect of the profession probing several promising routes into the future.

With respect to approval plans, what is needed now is a solid body of research, which will calm some of the controversy by moving us from opinion and prejudice into documented facts. In short, we need more than the profession's traditional crutch of self-evident truths or recourse to majority opinion to justify what we are doing. We need not, perhaps, go quite as far as a participant in last year's seminar suggested and establish an agency similar to the Library Technology Project to study all aspects of this technique of building research collections, but surely those of us who are convinced of both the efficiency and effectiveness of approval plans would do well to follow Thoreau's advice (slightly paraphrased): "You have built your castles in the air. Now put foundations under them."

Research into the operation of approval plans, though slim in terms of the general interest in the subject, does exist. For instance, for several years, the University of Nebraska has gathered detailed statistics on the number of titles received, the breakdown by LC class, average prices, and discounts. Florida Atlantic University has been compiling a similar data

bank on its computer since 1968. The University of Oklahoma Library has produced a solid vendor performance
study, of major significance, which tested the Abel Company's claim "that monographs eligible for coverage under
the Abel Approval Plan would be sent within the same week
of publication, and that 80 percent of these would be received before the title's first appearance in one of the trade
bibliographies."[1] Finally, there has been at least one disserta-
tion in which approval plans have come under scrutiny. I
refer to the work of Gayle Edward Evans at the University of
Illinois, comparing the use of books received through approval plans and those ordered individually by librarians and
members of the faculty.[2]

Much of the published and unpublished research on approval plans and the verbal exchanges between proponents
and opponents shares the common attribute of viewing approval plans largely in isolation from the total acquisitions
and processing effort. This is analogous to designing a power-
ful new automobile engine without facing up to the necessity
of also redesigning the entire drive train if the desired level of
performance is to result. The present study avoids this pitfall,
as much of the data on approval plans per se has been
extracted from a research project much larger in scope—a
unit cost study of the technical services divisions of five of
the seven libraries in the state university system of Florida
covering operations for fiscal 1968/69. The goal of the study
was to measure both efficiency (the optimal use of human

1. Kathleen Maher, Diana Lane, Martha Schmidt, and Charles Townley, *How Good Is Your Approval Plan, A Vendor Performance Study* (University of Oklahoma Libraries, 1969).

2. Gayle Edward Evans, "The Influence of Book Selection Agents Upon Book Collection Usage in Academic Libraries" (Ph.D. diss., University of Illinois, 1969).

resources), and effectiveness (the level of achievement in terms of established program goals).

The methodology of the study was as follows:

1. Each department of the technical services division defined in the clearest possible terms the functions for which it was responsible.
2. A diary study was carried out for each position in each department in order to distribute salary/wages and hours worked over the functions performed.
3. The total dollars and minutes spent on each function over a year's operation were then divided by the total volumes fully processed by the division.

Here it should be noted that the project was not a true time and motion study; it was not intended to be. The object was to determine the average costs per function, rather than the determination of a standard time per unit produced. Put another way, we wanted to determine how much it cost to acquire and process a book, including the costs of inefficient supervision, rather than what it should cost.

When this project was completed, data were available that made it possible, within reasonable limitations, to isolate cost factors related to books acquired through approval plans and those acquired in the traditional manner, and to come to some conclusions as to the relative efficiency of both techniques. In order to measure the impact of an approval plan on a library's level of achievement in terms of its established program goals, a supplementary study was undertaken, which was designed to test the effectiveness of an approval plan in expediting current published scholarship to the academic community.

From the unit cost studies of the five participating libraries, three functions were clearly identified which could be eliminated by utilizing an approval plan: pre-order searching; vendor selection; and typing purchase orders. Unfortunately, not all of the five libraries isolated each of the above functions in their studies. Consequently, it was necessary in some instances to use the average costs in minutes and dollars. For instance, if only four of the five had isolated vendor selection, the average costs for these four would be used for the fifth.

Table 1 shows the savings achieved by the two libraries in the test group that were on approval plans, and the savings that could have been achieved by the other three had they been. Table 2 shows the savings that would have accrued to the state university system had all five libraries been on approval plans. Translated into positions, the dollar savings would provide approximately five or six clerical positions (the average clerical salary at FAU being $4,800 in 1969/70) for the five libraries. These figures, shown in Table 2, show that an approval plan, on the average, will save the time of approximately one-and-a-half full-time persons.

The range of possible savings between institutions is both interesting and significant. At the lower end of the scale, Florida Atlantic University's figures were 1,073 man hours and $3,550. At the top, Library 3 could have saved double the number of hours and almost twice as much money as FAU had it been on an approval plan.

The greatest variation in costs was in preorder searching. Two factors apparently were operative. First, Libraries 2 and 4, which reported the highest costs, had more than one FTE professional assigned to this function. The two libraries with the lowest costs had no professional engaged in preorder

TABLE 1 SAVINGS ACHIEVED AT FAU AND LIBRARY 4 THROUGH AN APPROVAL PLAN AND THE SAVINGS WHICH COULD HAVE BEEN ACHIEVED BY THE THREE OTHER LIBRARIES IN THE TEST GROUP HAD THEY BEEN ON APPROVAL PLANS[a]

	Minutes Per Volume					Dollars Per Volume				
	Preorder Searching	Vendor Selection[b]	Typing P.O.'s	Per Vol Total	Total Savings 10,000 Vols[c]	Preorder Searching	Vendor Selection	Typing P.O.'s	Per Vol Total	Total Savings 10,000 Vols[d]
FAU	2.80	1.37	2.27	6.44	1,073	0.16	0.105	0.09	0.355	3,550
LIBRARY 1	2.20	1.67	6.53	10.40	1,733	0.12	0.14	0.19	0.45	4,500
LIBRARY 2	8.85	1.06	3.15	13.06	2,177	0.43	0.07	0.10	0.60	6,000
LIBRARY 3	7.75	1.06	6.87	15.98	2,663	0.38	0.07	0.23	0.68	6,800
LIBRARY 4[e]	9.70	1.37	4.13	15.20	2,533	0.38	0.105	0.12	0.605	6,050

[a]All data taken from a unit cost study of the Technical Services Division of five libraries in the state university system of Florida covering fiscal 1968/69.

[b]This function was not isolated in the unit cost studies at Florida and Library 4. The figures used are the average costs in minutes and dollars reported by two other libraries in the test group.

[c]Figures are for total hours.

[d]Figures are for total dollars.

[e]Had approval plans.

TABLE 2 SAVINGS WHICH COULD BE ACHIEVED FOR THE STATE UNIVERSITY SYSTEM OF FLORIDA IF ALL FIVE LIBRARIES INCLUDED IN THE STUDY UTILIZED AN APPROVAL PLAN OF 10,000 VOLUMES A YEAR[a]

Institution	Hours	Dollars
FAU	1,073	3,550
LIBRARY 1	1,733	4,500
LIBRARY 2	2,177	6,000
LIBRARY 3	2,663	6,800
LIBRARY 4	2,533	6,050
TOTAL	10,179	26,900

[a]Since over 95 percent of the titles received on an approval plan are single volumes, for the purpose of the study, titles and volumes are considered synonymous.

searching. At Florida Atlantic University, preorder searching was limited to determining if a given title actually existed. No attempt was made to establish the main entry before placing an order with a dealer. The other libraries in the test group followed the traditional procedure.

The spread in savings actual or potential between the five libraries illustrates an interesting paradox. The more efficient your bibliographic searching and acquisition procedures, the less likely you will be to save by having an approval plan, while the more inefficient they are, the greater will be your savings. The same situation holds true with respect to adjusted discounts; that is, calculating the discount on books received on an approval plan to include labor saved. Table 3 shows the results of computing the discount on approval-plan books on this basis for the five libraries which participated in the study. As can be seen, the adjusted discounts run from a low of just over 11 percent to a high of just over 14 percent. Either figure is highly respectable for an acquisitions program in excess of 10,000 volumes covering all areas of research.

The evidence derived from the unit cost studies undertaken by the five libraries of the state university system of Florida clearly supported the contention that the approval plan is an efficient method of acquiring current domestic scholarship. As the data showed, a well-managed approval plan can save, at the minimum, one full-time position, with significantly higher savings possible depending upon variances in internal procedures.

The vendor performance study carried out by the Univer-

TABLE 3 DEALER DISCOUNTS ON APPROVAL PLAN BOOKS CALCULATED TO INCLUDE LABOR DOLLARS SAVED THROUGH AN APPROVAL PLAN

FLORIDA ATLANTIC UNIVERSITY

Title purchased	10,000
Average price	$8.93
Average dealer discount	7.16%
Labor dollars saved per volume	
$3,550 - 10,000	$0.36
Additional discount	
$0.36 - $8.93	4%
Total adjusted discount	11.16%

Continued on page 11

TABLE 3 (CONTINUED)

LIBRARY 1

Titles purchased	10,000
Average price	$8.93
Average dealer discount	7.16%
Labor dollars saved per volume	
$4,500 − 10,000	$0.45
Additional discount	
$0.45 − $8.93	5%
Total adjusted discount	12.16%

LIBRARY 2

Titles purchased	10,000
Average price	$8.93
Average dealer discount	7.16%
Labor dollars saved per volume	
$6,000 − 10,000	$0.60
Additional discount	
$0.60 − $8.93	7%
Total adjusted discount	14.16%

LIBRARY 3

Titles purchased	10,000
Average price	$8.93
Average dealer discount	7.16%
Labor dollars saved per volume	
$6,800 − 10,000	$0.68
Additional discount	
$0.68 − $8.93	8%
Total adjusted discount	15.16%

LIBRARY 4

Titles purchased	10,000
Average price	$8.93
Average dealer discount	7.16%
Labor dollars saved per volume	
$6,050 − 10,000	$0.61
Additional discount	
$0.61 − $8.93	7%
Total adjusted discount	14.16%

12 / H. William Axford

sity of Oklahoma Libraries further bolsters the evidence for
the efficiency of approval plans. As already noted, the purpose of this study was to test the Abel Company's claim that
monographs eligible for coverage under the plan would be
sent within the week of publication, and that 80 percent of
these titles would arrive at the library before their first
appearance in a standard trade bibliography.

The team which carried out the research began by analyzing the fifteen issues of *Publishers Weekly* from August 28 to
December 2, 1968. These contained 8,977 titles. The team
concluded that 6,674 or 74 percent, fell within the exclusion
categories of the library's profile, and 2,303, or 26 percent,
within. Of the 2,303 which they felt should have been sent
by the dealer, 1,792, or 78 percent, were located in the
library's records; 509, or 22 percent, were not located. A
subsequent check reduced this latter figure to 466.

A list containing these 466 titles was forwarded to Abel's
Denver office to be checked. The district manager reported as
follows.

1. Of the titles on the list, 191 had been considered for
   inclusion on the approval plan but were rejected as being
   juvenile titles, items of local interest, or nonscholarly.
2. Two hundred seventy-five had been selected for the approval plan, and, of these, 111 were judged to fit the
   University of Oklahoma profile and had been shipped;
   133 were judged as not fitting the library's profile.
3. Thirty could not be accounted for.

The dealer's decisions for not sending certain titles were
based on the acquisitions librarian's instructions that the
library's profile was to be very strictly interpreted. In other
words, err in the direction of exclusion in case of doubt. It is

possible that the library's inclusion of 111 titles on the search list which had actually been sent under the approval plan may have been due to main entries on the invoices which differed from those in *Publishers Weekly* and paperbacks which may have been at the bindery and not located by the library during the study.

Subsequent correspondence on the results of the study between Abel's district manager and the director of the University of Oklahoma Libraries revealed a broad difference of opinion between the director's concept of what Abel should be sending and that of the acquisitions librarian. The latter's inclination was to narrow the coverage, the former's was to make it as broad as possible. Had Abel's Denver office operated under the director's interpretation of what should come under the libraries' profile, it is probable that the number of titles excluded would have been considerably smaller. This situation clearly illustrates a problem that often confronts the dealer. If the library assumes a Janus-like stance and speaks out of both mouths at once, the dealer can hardly be criticized if he fails to satisfy either. It also points out the managerial responsibilities inherent in an approval plan.

Adjusting the figures to take into account the 111 titles recorded as sent under the approval plan but apparently not located in the library at the time of the study, the Abel Company actually exceeded its claim to deliver 80 percent of the titles which fell within the week of publication and before their first appearance in a trade bibliography by 1.5 percent. The adjusted average early arrival was thirty-one days. After evaluating the evidence, the research team concluded "that the Abel All Books Plan is efficiently providing rapid delivery of current domestic publications to the University of Oklahoma Libraries."

As work progressed on our unit-cost studies, a vendor

performance study, similar to that done at Oklahoma, was undertaken. The methodology was to take a random sample of the titles received by the Florida Atlantic University Library through its approval plan during fiscal 1968/69 and check these in the public catalogs of four other university libraries in the state. The libraries in the test group were a private university that did not utilize an approval plan, a state university that did, a state university that did not, and a state university that had individual blanket orders with all university presses.

In fiscal 1968/69, the Florida Atlantic University Library accepted 10,648 titles through its approval plan. In January 1970, six months after the close of the fiscal year, this file was weeded to remove titles in series, corporate entries, and reprints. An 8 percent sample of the remaining 9,461 titles was then selected. Over the course of the next five months, the 764 titles obtained by this process were checked in the public catalogs of the libraries in the test group, the first one in January, two more in February, and the other in the first week of May. Since the Florida Atlantic University Library attempted to maintain a policy of giving original cataloging to all approval-plan books for which LC copy had not been received after ninety days, the bulk of the titles in the sample group had been fully cataloged by October 15, 1969. The time lags between this date and the dates when the catalogs of the libraries in the test group were checked were as follows: Institution 1, 10 weeks; Institutions 2 and 3, 14 weeks; Institution 4, 26 weeks.

The results of the catalog checks were unexpected and not easy to interpret. They are shown in Table 4.

Because of the very high percentage of titles not found in the public catalogs of the test group of libraries, university

TABLE 4 RESULTS OF CHECKING AN 8 PERCENT SAMPLE OF APPROVAL-PLAN BOOKS RECEIVED BY FAU DURING 1968/69 IN THE PUBLIC CATALOGS OF FOUR UNIVERSITY LIBRARIES IN FLORIDA

		Level[a]			Total	
	2	3	4	5	(No.)	(%)
Institution 1						
Not found	38	1,113	1,550	2,662	4,362	56.2
Older editions found	0	75	125	125	325	3.4
On order	0	0	0	0	0	0
Institution 2						
Not found	38	950	1,162	1,750	3,900	40.8
Older editions found	0	138	50	88	276	2.9
On order	0	288	400	1,061	1,749	18.3
Institution 3						
Not found	38	1,288	1,688	3,250	6,264	65.6
Older editions found	12	175	63	188	438	4.6
On order	0	0	0	0	0	0
Institution 4						
Not found	38	750	838	1,288	2,913	30.5
Older editions found	0	63	75	138	276	2.9
On order	0	38	38	50	126	1.3

[a] Abel Company's assigned level.

press titles and titles from a selected group of individual publishers noted for scholarly publication were studied separately. A slightly different pattern emerged, which again raised as many questions as it answered. For instance, at Library 2, which had individual blanket orders with all uni-

versity presses, the percentage of titles not held in the university press group was almost 10 percent higher than for the
whole list. Incredible as it may seem, this library lacked over
50 percent of the university press titles which had been
cataloged several months previously at Florida Atlantic University. On the other hand, the percentage of titles not held
for McGraw-Hill publications was only 6.9 percent.

In order to find out if the libraries not on approval plans
were acquiring university press titles by traditional techniques, these titles were separated into two groups: those
received during the first half of the fiscal year and those
received during the second half. At all institutions, the number of titles not held in the first group was substantially
lower than in the second. This finding seemed to indicate
clearly that the university press titles, which Florida Atlantic
had received through its approval plan, were being acquired
by traditional acquisitions procedures, but at a considerably
later date. Tables 5-8 show the results of this part of the
study in detail.

In attempting to interpret the data derived from the
catalog checks, several points must be remembered. First,
neither Library 1 nor Library 3 filed "on order" information
in their public catalog, nor did they file temporary entries for
titles in cataloging backlogs. Consequently, it is entirely possible that many of the titles not found in the catalog checks
were actually owned by these libraries, but not available to
the public. Many were probably on order. Although it would
have been desirable to obtain this information, not having it
does not really affect the overall findings of the study, which
revealed a very large number of scholarly titles not available
to the academic communities served by these two libraries
ten to fourteen weeks after they were available at Florida
Atlantic University. In the case of university press titles

TABLE 5 RESULTS OF CHECKING UNIVERSITY PRESS BOOKS RECEIVED AT FAU THROUGH BLANKET APPROVAL PLAN IN FISCAL 1968/69 AND FULLY CATALOGED BY SEPTEMBER 15, 1969, IN THE PUBLIC CATALOGS OF FOUR OTHER UNIVERSITY LIBRARIES IN FLORIDA[a]

Number of University Press Titles Received and Cataloged by FAU: 2,137

Number of Titles in This Group *Not* in the Public Catalogs of the Four Other University Libraries in Florida at the Time Checked.

	Titles	
Institution	(No.)	(%)
1[b]	975	45.6
2[c]	1,075	50.3
3[d]	1,325	62.0
4[e]	413	19.3

[a] All figures based on an 8 percent sample of 9,461 titles. All approval plan books for which LC copy was not available after ninety days were given original cataloging at FAU.

[b] Catalog checked in January 1970.

[c] Catalog checked in February 1970. Had standing orders with individual university presses.

[d] Catalog checked in February 1970.

[e] Catalog checked in May 1970. Had blanket approval plan.

received during the first half of the fiscal year, the time lag was from twenty-four to forty weeks.

Libraries 2 and 4 both filed "on order" information in the public catalog, and both filed temporary entries for all titles not cataloged. The "on order" information provided some

TABLE 6 RESULTS OF CHECKING PRAEGER, WILEY, MACMILLAN, PRENTICE-HALL, AND MCGRAW-HILL TITLES RECEIVED AT FAU THROUGH BLANKET APPROVAL PLAN DURING FISCAL 1968/69 AND FULLY CATALOGED BY SEPTEMBER 15, 1969, IN THE PUBLIC CATALOGS OF FOUR OTHER UNIVERSITY LIBRARIES IN FLORIDA[a]

Number of Titles Received and Cataloged from These Publishers by FAU

Praeger	275
Wiley	224
Macmillan	174
Prentice-Hall	225
McGraw-Hill	187

Number of Titles in This Group *Not* in the Public Catalogs of the Four Other Institutions at the Time Checked.

INSTITUTION	Praeger Titles		Wiley Titles		Macmillan Titles		Prentice-Hall Titles		McGraw-Hill Titles	
	(No.)	(%)	(No.)	(%)	(No.)	(%)	(No.)	(%)	(No.)	(%)
1[b]	175	63.6	125	55.8	88	50.5	125	55.5	75	40.1
2[c]	113	41.1	75	33.4	75	43.1	125	55.5	13	6.9

TABLE 6 (Continued)

INSTITUTION	Praeger Titles (No.)	(%)	Wiley Titles (No.)	(%)	Macmillan Titles (No.)	(%)	Prentice-Hall Titles (No.)	(%)	McGraw-Hill Titles (No.)	(%)
3[d]	136	49.4	125	55.8	63	36.2	150	66.6	113	60.4
4[e]	13	4.7	0	0	50	28.7	75	33.3	38	20.3

[a] All figures based on an 8 percent sample of 9,461 titles. All approval plan books for which LC copy was not available after ninety days were given original cataloging at FAU.

[b] Catalog checked in January 1970.

[c] Catalog checked in February 1970. Had standing orders with individual university presses.

[d] Catalog checked in February 1970.

[e] Catalog checked in May 1970. Had blanket approval plan.

TABLE 7 RESULTS OF CHECKING UNIVERSITY PRESS BOOKS RECEIVED AT FAU THROUGH BLANKET APPROVAL PLAN JULY 1, 1968 - DECEMBER 31, 1968, AND FULLY CATALOGED BY APRIL 15, 1969, IN THE PUBLIC CATALOG OF FOUR OTHER UNIVERSITY LIBRARIES IN FLORIDA[a]

Number of University Press Titles Received and Cataloged by FAU: 1,050

Number of Titles in This Group *Not* in the Public Catalogs of the Four Other University Libraries in Florida at the Time Checked.

Institution	Titles	
	(No.)	(%)
1[b]	387	36.8
2[c]	412	39.2
3[d]	575	54.7
4[e]	150	14.2

[a]All figures based on an 8 percent sample of 9,461 titles. All approval plan books for which LC copy was not available after ninety days were given original cataloging at FAU.
[b]Catalog checked in January 1970.
[c]Catalog checked in February 1970. Had standing order with individual university presses.
[d]Catalog checked in February 1970.
[e]Catalog checked in May 1970. Had blanket approval plan.

very positive documentation for the effectiveness of an approval plan. At Library 2, which had individual blanket-order plans with all university presses, 18.3 percent, or 1,749 titles, on the Florida Atlantic list were found to be on order. At Library 4, which had an approval plan, the figure dropped to 1.3 percent, or 126 titles. It is interesting, but somewhat confusing to note that both libraries missed exactly the same

TABLE 8 RESULTS OF CHECKING UNIVERSITY PRESS BOOKS RECEIVED AT FAU THROUGH BLANKET APPROVAL PLAN JANUARY 1, 1969 - JUNE 30, 1969, AND FULLY CATALOGED BY SEPTEMBER 15, 1969, IN THE PUBLIC CATALOGS OF FOUR OTHER UNIVERSITY LIBRARIES IN FLORIDA[a]

Number of University Press Titles Received and Cataloged by FAU: 1,087

Number of Titles in This Group *Not* in the Public Catalog of the Four Other University Libraries in Florida at the Time Checked.

Institution	Titles (No.)	(%)
1[b]	587	54.0
2[c]	662	63.0
3[d]	750	68.9
4[e]	262	24.1

[a]All figures based on an 8 percent sample of 9,461 titles. All approval plan books for which LC copy was not available after ninety days were given original cataloging at FAU.

[b]Catalog checked in January 1970.

[c]Catalog checked in February 1970. Had standing orders with individual university presses.

[d]Catalog checked in February 1970.

[e]Catalog checked in May 1970. Had blanket approval plan.

number of new editions of titles for which they held the previous edition (see Table 4).

It seems obvious that the approval plan technique for building research libraries is here to stay. The results of the present study clearly demonstrate its efficiency and effectiveness.

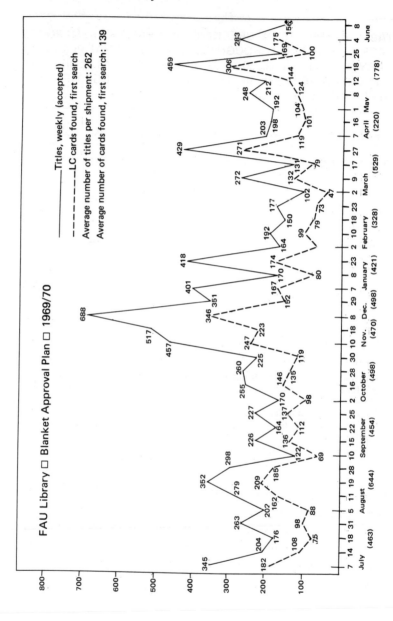

FAU Library □ Blanket Approval Plan □ 1969/70

Titles, weekly (accepted)
LC cards found, first search
Average number of titles per shipment: 262
Average number of cards found, first search: 139

TABLE 9 FLORIDA ATLANTIC UNIVERSITY LIBRARY TITLE II DEPOSITORY CARDS FOR BLANKET APPROVAL PLAN BOOKS, JANUARY-JUNE 1970

Shipment	Titles Accepted	LC on First Search	Titles Put On Hold	LC Copy Found on Second Search (30 days)	LC Copy Found on Third Search (60 days)	LC Copy Found on Fourth Search (90 days)	Number of Titles Without LC Copy After 90 Days
January 7	401	167	234	15	3	9	207
January 23	418	174	244	6	3	5	230
February 2	164	74	90	7	8	4	71
February 10	192	99	93	5	4	3	81
February 18	150	79	71	9	1	2	59
February 23	177	73	104	7	7	0	90
March 2	102	47	55	5	8	4	58
March 9	272	132	140	5	2	1	132
March 17	131	79	52	10	7	1	34
March 27	429	271	158	10	2	5	141
April 7	203	119	84	6	5	2	71
April 16	198	101	97	6	25	8	68
May 1	192	104	88	7	24	2	55
May 8	248	124	124	6	2	1	115
May 12	212	144	68	14	7	10	39
May 18	459	306	153	7	6	10	130
May 25	169	100	69	11	9	5	34
June 4	283	175	108	4	2	4	98
Average	262	139	113	8	7	4	95

2

Adopting an Approval Plan for a College Library: The Macalester College Experience

Daniel Gore

University libraries moving into approval-plan buying have often done so at a time when large amounts of new money were added to the book budget, permitting approval purchases to be added on top of the customary acquisitions program. Old habits were thus left largely undisturbed: retrospective collection development continued at the usual pace, and departmental allocation of book funds was modified only slightly, if at all. And even under such favorable conditions as these, as speakers at the first two of these seminars have testified, transition to approval buying may arouse fierce resentments among professors and librarians who cleave to the old myth that only they are truly qualified to select books for their library.

If the transition is made, as we had to make it, at a time when virtually the entire book budget must be committed to approval buying—leaving nothing for retrospective purchases or departmental allocations—one may expect to deal with passions of epic magnitude, unless one can offer some satisfactory options when proposing a moratorium on retrospective buying and departmental allocations.

For a college library of modest size, such as Macalester's (around 200,000 volumes), the only alternative to spending heavily each year on retrospective purchases is to offer the clientele ready and convenient access to someone else's retrospective collection, preferably one that is ten or fifteen times larger, so everyone will perceive the futility of attempting to duplicate it. When that is done, the sense of urgency regarding retrospective buying largely disappears.

Long before the idea of approval buying was hinted at to the Macalester faculty, we installed a courier service to fetch from the libraries of the University of Minnesota any book or journal article that was not available at Macalester. The courier is a staff member and makes a trip to the university libraries regularly five times a week, usually delivering requested items within about twenty-four hours. No charge is made for the service—not even for photocopies of journal articles—and, in some respects, it is even more convenient to use than our own library. Volume of requests is about four or five hundred items per month, and the success rate appears to be leveling off at around 70 percent. The service proved so popular, and so gratifying—even to those who made no use of it—that when the time came to propose at least a temporary moratorium on retrospective buying, most of the resistance in that area had already evaporated. Where it still persisted, little argument was required to convince holdouts that the courier service in itself accomplished more than several centuries of retrospective buying at our customary levels would do. The option offered was obviously many times better than the one it replaced, while the cost of it is substantially less. Without the courier service, I doubt the faculty would ever have agreed to call a halt—even a temporary one—to retrospective purchasing. Why should they, if that is their only convenient way of access to noncurrent publications?

A solution to the problem of suspending departmental allocations was not so easily arrived at. While most of the department chairmen were willing to experiment with approval buying, and some were even eager to do so, there were several whose resistance remained intractable, since they felt that their departments might receive fewer or less suitable books than in the past if they lost control of their allocations. There was no lessening of resistance when they discovered that, in point of fact, the allocation process had been utterly meaningless in the past, since only one-fifth of the book funds was actually allocated, with the other four-fifths going into what amounted to a librarian's discretionary fund.

While the library committee had strongly endorsed approval buying in principle after hearing presentations by two competing dealers, they had done so with the understanding that no action would be taken until general consent of the department chairmen had been obtained. Given the intransigence of several chairmen, I recommended to the committee that we abandon for the present any orthodox program of approval buying and offer instead an option based on departmental allocations. The specific proposal was this:

1. That the entire book budget be allocated by departments, according to whatever formula or other method the library committee finds appropriate;
2. That a complete approval profile of the college's requirements for current imprints be drawn up;
3. That departments be notified, on the basis of their profiled needs, when books are published that are likely to be of interest to them;

4. That departments may spend all, none, or a portion of their allocated funds to purchase books that match their profiled needs;
5. That when a department's allocated funds have been fully expended, no futher purchases may be made until the next fiscal year.

There being no objection to this proposal from any department chairman, the library committee adopted it with alacrity, not realizing the difficulties that lay ahead in making fair and reasonable allocations to departments. The difficulties were going to be far worse than they might have been ordinarily, since there were no legitimate precedents to follow. The only local tradition they had to guide them was the practice of allocating only a fifth of the funds, and leaving the remainder to the librarian's discretion. They saw no virtue in adhering to that custom, and neither did I, since its effect was to place in the hands of one person full authority for distributing book purchases over all areas of interest. The defects of such an arrangement were too obvious for argument or even comment, and the committee found themselves in the awkward position of having to create some rational means of allocating book funds; some rational means, that is, other than a strictly controlled program of profile buying as originally proposed.

The committee's first approach to the problem was to ask me to submit a summary description of allocation methods commonly practiced in other academic libraries. There was some hope that it might be easier to start with the writing on someone else's tablet and erase what is unsuitable than to start with a *tabula rasa* and try to write something sensible of one's own devising. I gave them a list of the various methods

practiced elsewhere, and told them I held no personal prefer-
ence for any one of them. The list I presented follows.

1. Follow percentages employed in past years, making
whatever adjustments seem appropriate in the light of changing programs, etc. Impossible in our situation, since we do
not know, and cannot find out, what the actual allocations
were.

2. Base allocation on various enrollment statistics, e.g.,
number of students taking departmental offerings, number of
departmental majors, honors students, independent study
programs, etc. Problem here is that, e.g., five classics students
may need access to more titles than five hundred physics
majors. Enrollment statistics are probably meaningful only in
terms of the number of multiple copies that should be
bought, but allocated funds are usually spread over as many
titles as possible.

3. Base allocation on circulation activity by subject. Thus,
if circulation in history is twice that in literature, allocate
twice as much to history. This method makes some sense, but
commits library development to the past rather than the
future. Subjects of no interest last year may become vitally
interesting this year or next, but new books will not be
available to satisfy the developing interest until circulation
activity leads to their purchase. By then, interest may have
died again. A further problem is that hand-kept circulation
statistics are not sufficiently detailed to be matched against
departmental allocations. Thus, while we can tell how many
books were circulated in the sciences this fall, and how many
in literature, we cannot tell how many were circulated in the
specific categories of biology, chemistry, physics, etc., or
English literature, French, German, Spanish, etc.

4. Develop an elaborate mathematical formula based on

some or all of the above subjective methods, announce that
the formula is an objective method of allocating funds, and
tell those who complain of the results that they simply
cannot grasp complex, abstract formulations.

5. Ask each department chairman to indicate how much
money for books he thinks his department will require, and
then begin negotiations if the aggregate exceeds 100 percent
of the available funds.

6. Determine allocation percentages at similar institutions,
establish an average, and follow it. The blind leading the
blind.

7. Determine last year's worldwide production of books,
distributed by subject, and distribute book funds in the same
proportion. Has same defects as point 3 above; furthermore,
it is impossible to determine the total production count, let
alone the distribution.

As a guide to their labors in developing a rationale for
allocating funds, the committee found this summary no more
helpful than a communication from the Delphic oracle. After
debating the options at some length, and trying in vain to
imagine some others that might be missing from the list, the
committee grew visibly frustrated by the irrational results
that might be expected to lie at the end of any path they
followed. As the frustrations mounted, and the solution to
one paradox led to the discovery of two new ones to take its
place, the committee began a drift toward approval-plan
buying as the only practical escape from the paradoxes of
departmental allocations; and the drift soon turned into a
stampede back to their earlier recommendation that the bulk
of the book funds be committed to orthodox buying based
on an approval-type profile. In less than an hour, they had
voted to rescind their recommendation that departments be

permitted to buy in or out of profile as they wished. At a subsequent meeting, they adopted a lengthy, carefully drawn set of resolutions submitted by a philosophy professor, stipulating that there would be no departmental allocations, and that, with a few necessary but minor exceptions, book funds would hereafter be expended on the basis of notification slips generated by a comprehensive profile of our current acquisition requirements. The committee left everyone with the clear impression that they had ceased to make recommendations and were now giving instructions of a kind the library was bound to follow. Opposition to the program seems to have collapsed with that development, and no further objections have since been heard, although some may well arise when full-scale implementation takes place.

This reversal of direction took me totally by surprise. I had not even speculated on such a possibility, although in retrospect it appears to be the best possible way to move into an approval program, since any residual hostility toward it may now be deflected toward the whole committee and away from the individual librarian who originally proposed the program. The outcome of these unforeseen changes of direction calls to mind Hamlet's observation that "there's a divinity that shapes our ends, rough-hew them how we will," although some of our faculty may see the devil's hand at work in it.

There is a third problem of a quite general nature, one that I did not mention earlier, that must be faced when the decision is taken to adopt an approval plan. The problem, touched on at the previous seminar, is this. Since a high percentage of approval purchases will reach the library before LC catalog copy is available, the advantage of early receipt of books may be largely dissipated by virtue of their simply sitting longer than usual on the processing shelves, awaiting the arrival of LC copy. Expediting the acquisition process aggravates the problem of cataloging backlogs. On top of this problem, we had the additional one of lacking any automatic system of matching books to catalog copy when both have finally reached the library. If you maintain a current proofslip file, with approval slips interfiled in it, the problem solves itself, for no matter which comes first—the proofslip or the approval slip—a match occurs automatically, without the need for systematic review either of proofslip files or approval receipts. But with acquisitions rates of about 7,000 titles per year, the sorting and filing of about 150,000 proofslips seems an unwarranted amount of labor to achieve only 7,000 matches (or less) with approval slips. The alternative of making repeated searches of NUC supplements for catalog copy would be exceedingly cumbersome, as would the other option of ordering cards from the Library of Congress when a book is received. And the problem of extended cataloging delays would not be resolved by any of these measures. We needed a method that would at once eliminate the occasions for proofslip files, multiple searches in NUC, and protracted delays in cataloging.

The method we finally developed is based on the principle of the "cataloging frontlog," apparently first tested by Marvin Scilken at the Orange, New Jersey, Public Library, and described by him in the September 15, 1969, *Library Journal*. We call our system the FASTCAT, and it works like this. The day a new book is received in the library, its order number is typed on a pressure-sensitive label, with the designator FASTCAT above it; the label is fastened to the spine of the book, and it is immediately placed in the FASTCAT collection (in our main reading room) where it is ready to circulate. Books in this collection are naturally arranged by order number (which is also the control number for circulation purposes), so the shelf-order of books approximates the order in which they are received. The lower the FASTCAT number, the older the book.

How does one know that a particular book is on FAST-CAT shelves, and what its FASTCAT call number is? This information is available from the title section of the card catalog, where a copy of each book's order form remains until the book is permanently cataloged. When a book arrives, a tape is attached to the order form indicating the book is available, and one can tell by glancing at the order number what the book's call number will be on the FASTCAT shelves.

FASTCAT books are left on the FASTCAT shelves for six months or longer, allowing time for most LC copy that will ever appear to be printed in the quarterly NUC supplements. After this minimum aging time has elapsed, a group of FASTCAT books is removed from the shelves and searched in NUC. When copy is found, it is enlarged directly on a Minolta photocopy machine, and, from this copy, sets of catalog cards are produced on a Xerox machine. If LC copy is not found at this time, the book is returned to the FASTCAT shelves and left there for another six months or a year, when a second search will be made. If the second search proves negative, the book is custom cataloged and sent on its way.

Under this arrangement, all approval receipts can be circulated the day they arrive, all pressures for rush cataloging are removed, and all cataloging backlogs are eliminated. For most books, a single search in NUC yields the desired copy, and, for a small remnant, a second search concludes the operation. Without such a method as this for prompt circulation and efficient cataloging of approval receipts, approval-plan buying would be far less attractive to us. No claim is made here for the suitability of the FASTCAT operation in university libraries, where the existence of numerous branches poses problems of another order than those a small college library faces. For libraries such as Macalester's, the FASTCAT operation appears to be the method of choice for relieving the cataloging presssures generated by earlier-than-usual receipt of approval books.

A word now about that term "approval," which somehow stirs dark passions in the hearts of some professors and some librarians. In the acquisitions program we have set up, it is a misnomer, since we are not actually buying books on an approval basis. Instead, we are receiving computer-produced notification slips from the jobber, based on a comprehensive profile of our acquisitions requirements. Books not wanted are not ordered; books ordered are kept, since further review of them on any kind of approval basis would be useless. We therefore speak of our program as a "profile plan" rather than an "approval plan," and have discovered that the shift in terminology has, in fact, removed some of the purely emotional biases against the program.

One problem of profile buying that bedevils both university librarians and their jobbers is the handling of monographs in series. University libraries feel obliged to acquire all titles in a great many series, with no exceptions tolerated; and the process of transferring their standing order files to the profile jobber is cumbersome, costly, and complicated by numerous difficulties of timing and communication. Since we regard the standing-order monographic series as an inappropriate selection device for a small college library, we simply canceled all such standing orders and instructed the jobber to notify us of titles that match our profile, without regard to any series identification they may carry. Thus, if six titles out of ten in a given monographic series fit our profile, we will acquire only those six, worrying no more about those other four than we would any other books that lay outside the profile. The problem of identifying on receipt new monographs that should be placed in an existing series is largely settled by classing nearly all monographs separately hereafter, regardless of any series relationship that may exist. While such a Draconian solution to the problem may appear to have many theoretical defects, it is difficult to find any practical faults with it, at least in a college-library situation. Six months ago, we removed all monographic series added entries from the public catalog, and no one but the cataloger is yet aware that anything is missing.

How well is the profile program working for us now? It is too early to say, as we have been receiving slips for only a month. Our major concern at this stage is that the profile receipts not exceed the sum available for their purchase (about $70,000 per year), or, what would be equally troublesome, that they not fall substantially short of the budgeted amount. In the latter event, we might find ourselves in the allocation dilemma again, and without sufficient time to settle it before the end of the fiscal year. The jobber assures us of his keen interest in forestalling any such development. I am sure he will be able to.

POSTSCRIPT

Gross statistical results of the first six months, January - June 1971, of profile buying follow:

	Number	Dollars	Average Cost per Volume
Notice slips received from jobber	4,719	44,153	$9.35
"Yes" slips returned by faculty	2,112	17,641	8.35
"No" slips returned by faculty	1,598	17,034	10.60
Total "yes" and "no" slips returned	3,710	34,675	
Percentage "yes"	57	51	
Percentage "no"	43	49	
Notice slips not yet acted on by faculty	1,009	9,478	

It appears that a full year's operation will yield notices covering about 9,400 titles, costing $88,000. Of these, the faculty will elect to buy 5,350, costing $44,000. The average per-volume costs suggest that the faculty may be taking price into account as a selection criterion, since the average cost of the volumes they reject is 25 percent greater than for those they accept. The 43 percent rejection rate (based on *number* of titles) is a good deal higher than I would have forecast, and certainly much beyond what the jobber could tolerate with the conventional approval arrangement.

3

Total Effect of Approval Plans on the Nation's Academic Libraries

David O. Lane

This paper is based on a questionnaire mailed last spring to the seventy-seven academic library members of the Association of Research Libraries. In some ways, this questionnaire was a repeat of one Carl White and I circulated to a similar group of libraries in 1969. That questionnaire was a preliminary to a presentation at a HEW sponsored institute at University of California at San Diego in September 1969.

The questionnaire on which this paper is based consisted of fifteen questions, many of a simple "yes/no" nature. As several respondents commented, some of the questions could not be completely answered by a yes or no; I was aware of this, but felt a rather simple questionnaire built in this way and emphasizing such qualifying words as "estimate," "approximate," "in general," etc., had a greater chance of being answered by more libraries. It is my experience that too detailed a questionnaire is likely not to be answered at all. Most libraries responded to the questions in the proper light, and I believe the resulting data, though no doubt not specific to the third decimal point, give us a good picture of the importance today of approval plans, blanket orders, and other gathering plans to the academic research libraries of North America.

The data gathered are interesting, but possibly were not worth collecting again at this time as it had been done before, most recently, I expect, by Norman Dudley of University of California, Los Angeles, for his article "The Blanket Order" which appeared in the January 1970 issue of *Library Trends*. In all truthfulness, this questionnaire would have been quite different if I had seen that article before it was mailed out, almost one year ago now. However, I did not read the Dudley paper until about two weeks later. If nothing else, it is of interest to note the continuity of results between my earlier effort, Norman Dudley's of a year ago, and this paper.

At the same time, I did have a more important consideration in mind in constructing this questionnaire. I wished to form a data base and a chain of thought leading up to question 14. This question had been suggested to me by Peter Spyers-Duran as an interesting concept to investigate. I suppose most of us who have had any conversations concerning approval and blanket plans, especially as offered by two or three major jobbers in this nation and important dealers in England, France, and Germany, have had to consider this point; certainly it has been brought up often enough by opponents of such plans. In effect, this opinion holds that the major academic research libraries of North America, by utilizing the services of a small number of jobbers and dealers, are building book collections that are too similar in both strengths and weaknesses. It was in order to find out what our major academic research libraries thought of this that the ARL institutions were selected for study.

Now for the results. Of the seventy-seven libraries approached, fifty-nine (76.6 percent) replied—a very respectable return.

Question 1 reads: "Does your library participate in any kind of automatic approval, gathering or blanket order, or other acquisition plan?" Five replied no, fifty-four replied yes (91½ percent). Of these fifty-four affirmative replies, I have grouped eight together as having only marginal plans; that is, they spend from $25.00 to $5,000.00 annually for gathering-plan acquisitions.

Question 2 reads: "If Yes, what kind of program (check as appropriate): approval plan, gathering plan, other. If other, please describe." Of the fifty-four institutions utilizing gathering plans, thirty indicated that they maintained some sort of approval plan and twenty-three operate blanket-order plans. A few replies were not classifiable for the purpose of this paper.

Question 3 was concerned with the major gathering plans in operation at the various libraries and the languages of publications received. At thirty-two libraries, the majority of volumes received were in English; at twenty-two, the majority were in foreign languages. Several libraries pointed out that they operate several plans, and many languages were represented by sizable receipts. This I expected. However, I find the correlation between approval plans (thirty) and major language, English (thirty-two), on one hand and gathering plans (twenty-three) and majority of receipts in foreign languages (thirty-two) quite interesting.

Question 4 was concerned with the languages, other than English, prominently represented in the volumes gathered. The replies were as follows:

Language	Libraries Responding
German	19
Russian	12
French	11
Spanish	6
Italian	4
Arabic Indian Pakistani Hebrew Japanese	2 each
Chinese Portuguese Persian Turkish Indonesian	1 each

"Most all languages" was mentioned once, "the usual languages" once, "non-Western European languages" once, "all Western European languages" once, and "all major Western and Cyrillic languages" twice.

Question 5 reads as follows: "Please estimate the total annual expenditure of your library on automatic acquisition plans." The fifty-four libraries maintaining plans replied as follows. (Of the eight I deemed marginally involved, four answered, and these are shown in column 1. Column 2 gives the responses of libraries with plans resulting in a majority of English-language receipts, and column 3 represents those libraries whose major receipts are in foreign languages.)

Marginal	English-Language Majority		Foreign-Language Majority
$ 25	$20,000	100,000	$15,000
100	20,000	100,000	27,500
2,500	25,000	105,000	40,000
5,000	26,500	110,000	50,000
	51,000	113,000	78,500
	60,000	120,000	100,000
Average:	72,000	122,000	121,000
$1,906	75,000	125,000	150,000
	80,000	143,000	170,000
	80,000	150,000	200,000
	85,000	150,000	231,000
	88,500	150,000	300,000
	90,000		
	92,000		
	93,000	Average:	Average:
	95,000	$91,300	$123,583
	95,000		
	98,000		

Average of columns 2 and 3:
$100,524

Questions 6 asked, "What percentage of your total annual book funds (defined as expenditures for books, periodicals, microforms, etc., but excluding bindings) does this represent?" The figures reported for question 6 are below. Again, the replies are presented in three columns:

Marginal	English-Language Majority		Foreign-Language Majority
0.0008%	3%	12.22%	2.5%
1.00	5	14	3
1.38	5	14	5
	5.8	14	5
	7	14	10
	7	18	10
	7	18	11
	7	19.3	12
	8.74	20	12
	10	21.3	20
	10	23	20
	10	25	23
	10	25	35
	10	33	
	11	33	Average: 13%
		Average: 14%	Average of columns 2 and 3: 13.7%

Question 7 began a different line of investigation. It read: "Do you individually order titles that are requested by faculty or staff in those cases where you would expect the items to come to you on one or another of your automatic acquisition plans, but to date have not? Yes, at once; Yes, after the lapse of some time; No." Of the "majority English-language receipts," the replies were as follows:

At once	10
At once, if marked "rush"	2
After a lapse of some time	15
No	3

The replies from the "majority of foreign-language receipts" group were:

At once	1
At once, if marked "rush"	3
After a lapse of some time	10
No	2

Question 8 refers back to question 7: "If yes, from whom do you attempt to purchase such a title: a) the jobber or dealer who handles the appropriate subject area or language gathering plan for your library; b) other (please explain)." Again, I have arranged the answers by the language of the majority of receipts.

	Majority English	Majority Foreign
Appropriate jobber, dealer, etc.	18	13
As above, if foreign		2
Publisher	4	2
Other jobber or publisher so as to avoid confusion	4	
It depends	1	
Local store	1	

Questions 9 and 10 were a pair of related procedural questions. "Do you attempt, in any systematic manner, to check your receipts against the total bibliographic area or areas covered by your acquisition plans? If yes, please explain how. If no, why not?" Again, the replies are presented in a two-column arrangement:

	Majority English	Majority Foreign
Yes		
By checking *Publishers Weekly*, etc.	6	
Publishers' catalogs	1	
Against national bibliographies, etc.	2	9
No		
Can't afford	18	7
Spot checks only	1	
No, because if we miss a book and it is needed, someone will request it	1	
Not as yet (later)	1	

Question 11 was as follows: "Are you generally satisfied with the acquisitions plans now in operation at your library?" Of the group of forty-six libraries that were identified as having important gathering plans in operation, forty-three replied yes, two replied no, and one "too early to tell." Of the forty-three positive replies, twenty-seven were from what I have been referring to as the "majority of English-language receipts" group, as were the two "no's" and the one "too early to tell."

Questions 12 and 13 were related. "Do you intend to change the scope of your gathering plans in the foreseeable future, and if so, how?" Here I have again grouped the replies in three columns:

	Marginal Plans	Majority English-language Receipts	Majority Foreign Language
No	6	7	6
Yes			
In existing areas of coverage		4	
To other areas		16	8
Diminish existing coverage		1	1
Don't know	1	2	

In some ways, question 14 was the heart of the questionnaire. "It has been suggested that a major flaw in a large percentage of the academic libraries in this nation utilizing similar approval or standing order plans, all based on the work of a handful of jobbers or dealers, is that all such libraries would tend to collect about the same volumes, and at the same time miss the same important, but somehow jobber-overlooked, titles. Would you please comment on this?" In summarizing the replies, I have attempted, for purposes of correlation, to phrase a short response that seems to fit the intent of a group of more lengthy statements. Overall, of the fifty-four involved libraries, eleven tend to agree with the statement, two have no comment, and forty-one disagree. The high preponderance of disagreement with the opinion stated in question 14, including some well-reasoned statements, convinces me, at least, that this "majority flaw" need not be, and indeed, at present, is not a real problem. The summarized replies follow. Of the eight institutions that I have considered as being only marginally involved with such plans, four agreed with the statement, one made no comment, and three disagreed as follows:

> If additional books are needed, we would request them.
>
> No library would rely totally on this type of acquisitions procedure.
>
> This is an invalid argument.

Of the group that was identified as receiving a majority of English-language publications on their plans, five appeared to agree with the statement: one simply said "agree," three replied possibly so, and one last agreed, but added they had not the staff to do more. One library made no comment.

With respect to the group of libraries receiving a majority of foreign-language publications on their gathering plans, one simply agreed with the statement, while a second, though agreeing, added that this was why rigorous bibliographic checking of receipts against output was necessary.

This leaves the thirty-seven libraries with sizable gathering plans who disagreed with the statement being considered. Of these thirty-seven, twenty-four receive a majority of English-language publications (EL), while thirteen, a majority of foreign language items (FL). Their comments are summarized below:

> If only one jobber is used for all the acquisitions of a library, this might be so, but this is never the case. (15 El, 3 FL)

Not so, as any gathering plan must be monitored. (4 EL, 1 FL)

We see no problem. (5 FL)

Not so, as the time saved us through the use of gathering plans allows us to concentrate on tracking down the ephemeral items. (2 EL)

Not so, as selection is still in the hands of the library. (2 FL)

Not so with us. (2 EL)

Not so, as we realize that perfect coverage from any jobber is not possible. (1 FL)

Not so, as all library-interest profiles differ. (1 FL)

Any acquisitions librarian who relies solely on gathering plans is not doing a good job. (1 FL)

Here are direct quotes, both pro and con, from a few of the replies to this question:

This reasoning implies that the major selecting is being given over to the jobber. This is not so. The approval plan is basically an ordering device, whereby we obtain more quickly and economically books we would be ordering anyway. We will always have individual orders to be placed for the unusual, the out-of-print, the back volume. The use of approval plans will save time which can be spent on expanding the latter type of orders.

This is a danger, but it can be avoided if librarians remember that approval plans are only tools and, as such, require the guidance of an intelligent hand. Jobbers will take over library development only if librarians abdicate their responsibility, first to shape approval plans to meet their individual libraries' needs, then to supplement them as needed.

There will always be important titles which are missed. We feel that because of the approval plan we have more time to spend in searching out these important missing titles. Time which otherwise would have to be spent in . . . ordering hundreds of titles now supplied automatically through the approval plan.

Best use of these plans is to gather that material that will obviously be needed—and if this duplicates what another library gets, so what. You need it, too. The specialized material will have to be acquired either through very specialized approval plans or by good old-fashioned handpicking.

May I add my own personal highly subjective opinion on blanket orders? The librarian of a given institution knows, or should know, the strengths and weaknesses of his collections, the comparative standing of the various academic departments, and actual demand. He is also perhaps better qualified to guess what future demands are going to be than somebody else. Should the foregoing be an acceptable assumption, it is clear that the librarian is better qualified to do the book selection for his institution than any dealer or outsider for that matter.

I do believe this is very true. I prefer to do (or have the subject specialists do) individual selection. Also, our entire procedures, including automation, hinge on the order number for each title which is assigned when the book is selected for order.

Question 15 reads as follows: "I would appreciate any other comments you would care to make on any aspect of approval, standing order, and/or gathering plans." Many of the comments could be reduced to the following types of statements, repeated in some cases, by more than one respondent.

Serials and sets are problems with gathering plans.

We prefer to select our books!

Knowledgeable librarians can do a better job.

Approval plans can work, but material received *must* be reviewed.

Gathering plans are especially needed to collect the publications of developing nations.

Without the approval plan, we couldn't reasonably expend our book funds, due to a very small staff.

Approval and gathering plans have been popular, since it has been easier to get book funds than staff funds.

A few of the more interesting comments are quoted below:

They should have been "invented" decades ago. Our collections would not now be so spotty if they had.

Although in a minority, I firmly believe that English-language blanket or approval plans do not save time or money for large libraries, excepting university press blanket orders.

If vendors who offered approval plans would give the services they claim to give, these plans would be beneficial to all concerned.

Contrary to the opinion of some, libraries which have approval plans are not abdicating their responsibility for book selection. They have in fact strengthened their ability to do good book selection by having on hand for examination the materials on which they are passing judgment. Faculty acceptance of the approval plan at this university has been such as to make it almost impossible to go back to the old method of having faculty members request items for purchase.

We are disturbed that the discounts on books in the plans are being reduced in order to cover the costs of the jobber in supplying harder-to-get materials. We feel the jobbers should limit themselves to the original plan and not try to become all things to all people.

Our French blanket order can be considered successful as is the blanket order for German literature. German history is another matter and may be dropped. I can see no valid reason for an approval plan for U.S. imprints. We have talked to representatives but prefer to avoid approval plans.

I would assume, at least from the response to this questionnaire, that approval and gathering plans will be with us for some time to come. However, it is also obvious that they continue to be a subject of strenuous disagreement among the practitioners of book selection and collection development.

4

Why Approval Plans Fail

Mark M. Gormley

The approval plan has evolved as a cooperative effort between librarians and booksellers to help librarians acquire
those books which are needed to support the curriculum and
research programs of academic institutions. While most plans
cover scholarly works primarily, plans can be developed to
cover other types of literature as well. The main object is to
acquire all materials in a given field as they are published, at
the best possible price, and with maximum resultant savings
in library staff time. Put another way, the idea is to enable
the librarian to heed Dewey's admonishment to "get the right
book to the right person at the right time"—the fastest
possible time.

The main criticism of this automatic gathering of everything in a given area is that much "junk" is added along with
the good books. I think we must accept the premise that no
university library has to apologize for its collection, but it
can be castigated for what it does not have. Who here today
can prophesy what book is going to be good or bad ten years
from now? If the book is good, the library will have it and

not have to pay inflated prices in the out-of-print market, if the book is available at all. If it is bad, it can be discarded.

Considering the lack of in-depth study of approval plans, I can speak only from personal observation and experience. While plans are working with varying degrees of success around the country, very few are failing.

In libraries where plans have not succeeded, the reason can be laid on the same doorstep as the reason why most of them do work well, and that is the people involved: people—librarians and booksellers—who know and understand each other's aims and objectives. It is most imprudent for a librarian to try to operate a plan when the staff, who will do the work, is not fully apprised of the long-range projected accomplishments of the plan.

In 1967, I did a number of administrative surveys. Concerning the library in one small but rapidly growing university, I made the following observation to the president in my report:

> In a short visit of this nature, it is difficult to render an objective opinion on the adequacy of book collections. The librarian should systematically check into the holdings against standard bibliographies in the various disciplines. The filling of obvious gaps in the collection is a constant process in any library. Recent input of books has been good when one considers the size of staff and methods used. I think that the adoption of new methods for processing of materials will improve the input without a proportionate increase in staff size. I stress that this input must be increased substantially to meet the many new programs which are developing.

This was a case where the whole curriculum was spreading like a prairie grass fire, but collection development was not outrunning it, to say the least. Here is the "hooker" in the report: "The adoption of an automatic acquisitions program in selected areas will help greatly and acquisition of retrospective materials must increase at an accelerated pace." I hope I have learned to be careful in what I say. Let me repeat, "the adoption of an automatic acquisitions program in selected areas will help greatly." One sentence out of seven pages! Well, somebody noticed that point, and the school started an approval plan. The book budget was approximately $100,000.

At that very time, the library director left his job, and an acting director, who became a permanent director, was appointed for one year.

During the interregnum, the library contracted with a vendor, and the books started pouring in. The people—the staff—did not understand the concept, let alone the avalanche. The vendor evidently did not bother checking too carefully the results of the input. To make a long story short, by the end of the year about two years' budget was tied up in approval books. This plan failed miserably. The faculty went up in arms, naturally. The administration was very concerned. Subsequently, the library is acquiring, almost by rejection, new books published title by title. An unprepared, thinly staffed situation was not helped by this plan.

Mr. Rouse, at least year's conference, acquainted you with the situation at Oklahoma State: an incumbent director decided that the approval plan was good, but did not involve too many people on the staff in the decision.[1] The director departed, and disenchantment with the plan set in. Moral:

1. Roscoe Rouse, "Automation Stops Here," in Peter Spyers-Duran and Daniel Gore, eds., *Advances in Understanding Approval and Gathering Plans in Academic Libraries* (Kalamazoo: Western Michigan University, 1970), pp. 35-51.

never try out a plan when the staff is not fully apprised of long-range projections, and explain to the people who must make the plan work just what it is supposed to do.

I have heard Mr. Chapin at this conference say that, in his situation, people find it much more time-consuming to select a book with a book in hand than from printed bibliographies. What does this do for the book that does not hit the review medium for quite a while? Is *Publishers Weekly* all that good? I personally think that it's easier to judge an item with book in hand than from bibliographic or review sources. And it's more fun! There's no greater thrill in this business than going through new books.

Considering the concept of getting proper books into collections according to the library's profile, if it is determined that a selector is spending too much time perusing the title, then it is up to the acquisitions librarian or the director to boost things along.

Most of the acquisitions people and directors that I have talked to feel that, by and large, the plan, as far as getting the books from publisher through a vendor and into the library is concerned, is working very well. But I see a much bigger problem. I have seen large collections of current books backed up in receiving rooms.

The University of Wisconsin-Milwaukee Library takes great pride in the rapid speed with which books get on the shelves. When LC copy awaits the book the book is most often on the shelf within twenty-four hours. There is a six-month cutoff period to await LC copy before the book gets to original cataloging. At Wayne State, much the same pattern pertains. If LC copy is not immediately available, a copy of the order slip is filed as a brief-listed entry in the public catalog.

Those libraries that wait for LC copy to process a book must be careful. A survey done by Richard Abel & Co. four or five years ago indicated that a substantial percentage of English-language titles were not processed by LC at all. I suggest that a maximum time limit of six months be set for any title awaiting processing before the book receives original classification and cataloging.

Another problem in the approval plan is *who* really selects a title? In my present situation at Wayne State, there are four divisional librarians, two professional school librarians, and an acquisitions department. It is interesting to note that often there is disagreement among these experts on what title should or should not enter the collection. (The head acquisitions librarian acts as referee when necessary.)

I think there should be one person doing the selecting in the library. It takes a remarkable bookman. I hesitate to admit to this group the fact that these remarkable book people seem to be becoming fewer and fewer in librarianship. One person who has grasped the concept of the total academic program, who knows the total library collection, who knows the publishing business with its problems and price structure, can perform wonders in collection building. Mr. Spyers-Duran and I witnessed a transaction a couple of years ago which exemplifies my point. Our rejection rate for approval-plan books became alarmingly high in a very short period of time. The vendor was concerned to the point of delivering our weekly shipment personally. After the pleasantries were over, the boxes were opened As it happened, the deck was stacked against the vendor that day. The shipment contained German-language elementary texts, books older than our date limitation, and items on which we questioned the discount factor. The rejection rate that day was 75 percent. The reason was simple; a new employee of the vendor did not pay close enough attention to the limitations of the profile. The vendor must take responsibility to analyze carefully returns to help determine what is amiss. If he is getting a high rate of rejects—why? My point is that clear, quick, and immediate decision-making at the library expedited the acquisitions process.

I think that it is important to have a firm understanding with a vendor concerning a cutoff date. For example, 1970 imprints would not be accepted after April 1, 1971, even though we know that a few titles in preparation for publication with a 1970 imprint will not be released for a number of months. That problem constitutes another little exercise for our library book man. The problem of ordering duplicates and titles missed on the approval plan is easily solved by having a very good vendor in the approval business and another very good friend in the one-shot business.

It is definitely up to the library to define subject areas. It is up to the vendor to adhere as closely as possible to this profile. I will compliment, if I may, all of the large-scale vendors here for working out some very elaborate profile forms, everything from check sheets to computer-matched forms. I would caution the librarians that it is unfair to expect perfection on the part of the vendor, no matter how elaborate the form. There is always a margin for human error, and sometimes it is as simple as "you can't judge a book by its cover."

While we are all interested in making limited budgets go as far as possible, I have never considered the rather nebulous area of discounts to be a deciding factor in making purchase decisions. Much more important is consistently good service. A vendor knows what profit margin he must obtain if he is to stay healthy, and I will gladly help him provide it *if* he maintains excellent service.

Another problem that I have discussed over the last few years concerning approval plans is the cancellation of current standing orders. Most vendors will assume responsibility for canceling such standing-order plans. (There are exceptions.) Let me state that service thus provided is of great benefit to the library. I speak from personal experience. I consider it part of the service we are paying for.

Perhaps librarians are often lax in telling vendors about complaints: titles received which do not fit the profile, and (more important), titles not received. Communication both ways is so very important. I know that all of you in the book business welcome not only constructive complaints but the compliments that you more often deserve.

Reprints have been mentioned as a prime problem in large-scale gathering efforts. I know they can be, but here again, along with careful checking of catalogs, it takes that good bookman in the library to recognize a reprint. This is an area in which the divisional subject-matter specialists (and faculty) can be of big help. I might add that, in the larger collections, this problem of duplicating does not bother me too much. When considering the tremendous size of present-day student bodies and the physical condition of many of the original editions, I think it prudent to have the duplicate in many cases.

We all know that you people in the book business do have problems in identifying some titles, especially if you have a customer who wants you to furnish the output of minor presses. Some items never hit the standard reviewing agents or the standard bibliographic tools. In the larger libraries, this problem is best handled in-house.

I cannot overstress the importance of the profile. It will change as the university's needs change. While it must be the joint effort of both parties to make it operate, it is the librarian's job to define it. Not too many of us who direct libraries really know where the university is going insofar as special developments are concerned. A university is a surprisingly fluid entity, and few have written plans for the next ten years. From my observations, the approval-plan approach has been very well accepted by university faculties. It has taken some rather sophisticated selling by the librarian in some cases, but it appears that if he is doing a good job in building in-print collections, the faculty is glad enough to let him do it.

5

Internal Systems for Handling Approval Plans: A Case Study

LeMoyne W. Anderson

THE PROBLEM

A number of developments in higher education today bear directly upon a critical problem which academic librarians face. Students in the 1970s are probably more advanced academically than they were in the past; they are more physically mature; they are often married; an increasing number attend college; and a far larger percentage continue into graduate school— all of which leads to greater numbers making greater use of library resources. As the numbers increase, the demands for more materials rise correspondingly.

A collection must be assembled to meet these needs within the fiscal limitation of a particular institution's book budget. To accomplish this monumental task, furthermore, adequate numbers of staff must be on hand to select, acquire, organize, and prepare the material for the shelves. Experience has shown repeatedly, moreover, that while book funds may be readily available, the commensurate numbers of staff to handle the selection and processing may not be forthcoming.

58

If these are the problems, one fundamental question follows: are there manners and means to employ whereby the needs of the patron can be met at a minimum of time and effort expended by library personnel?

THE METHODOLOGY

Case Study

My report is essentially the result of a brief case study. The method followed was to gather all available information which had any possible connection with the life history and development of the handling of approval-plan materials at one library. It was predicted that after finishing this gathering of facts, the investigator would have a complete and continuous picture of the approval experiences over a period of time and, hopefully, could then make an interpretation.

It is realized that this method suffers from several defects. One is the difficulty of selecting a typical library. The second is the strong element of subjectivity which the investigator brings into the situation.

Assumptions and Definitions

In this study, certain assumptions were made. It is a premise of collection development at the institution under study that an academic library should acquire all current domestic scholarly monographs judged to be important in supporting the teaching and research programs. It is assumed, furthermore, that the selection decisions are principally the responsibility of a librarian. Decisions are not made unilaterally, but in concert with faculty and students.

For the purpose of this study, the definition of an approval plan is: "An arrangement whereby a dealer sends a library published material chosen according to individually tailored and mutually agreeable parameters; and, from this selection, the librarian, with the assistance of the faculty, examines the books in hand to determine which titles to retain and which to return."

The Site

The site of the investigation was Colorado State University. There are over 17,000 students currently pursuing programs in nearly a hundred areas at CSU, thirty-two of which lead to the doctorate. Much of the academic life revolved around the library. The present building was occupied in January 1965. It is a modular structure housing the current collection of nearly 800,000 volumes and a vast array of periodicals, journals, newspapers, manuscripts, films, phonodiscs, and other fugitive materials. This central facility accommodates over 2,000 readers.

The Technique

The principal technique of this investigation was to study and review uniformly the procedures that have developed in the handling of approval-plan materials within a library system. A step-by-step process was constructed in which interviews by the investigator with the principals were undertaken. In addition, observations were made over several separate days in order to inventory, as widely as possible, all elements in the processes. The steps were subsequently delineated after careful scrutiny. Attempts were made to keep the technique simple, knowing that the likelihood of accuracy would be increased. The probability of completeness seemed obvious if the techniques could be kept uniform and uncomplicated.

THE INTERNAL SYSTEM

One of the first tasks of the investigator was to establish a procedure by which the entire spectrum of activities within the approval-plan system could be conveyed. A few basic facts may help set the stage for the description of the system. First, let me outline the organization and the staff complement. Of 108 full-time equivalent positions, 55 are in the technical services division, which is divided into five major departments: acquisitions, identification, catalog, preparation, and documents (see Figure 1).

It should be emphasized that book selection is centered in the public services division— specifically among the several subject and reference librarians. All of the technical services departments, on the other hand, with the exception of documents, are welded into one link or another in the chain of events leading from selection to shelving of approval materials.

The Profile

The process of handling approval materials begins with development of the profile. The participants include the subject librarians coordinated by the assistant director of libraries for technical services, who, in a sense, serves as the chief bibliographer. After the subject profile has been developed, it is

FIGURE 1

Colorado State University Libraries
Technical Services Division Organization Chart

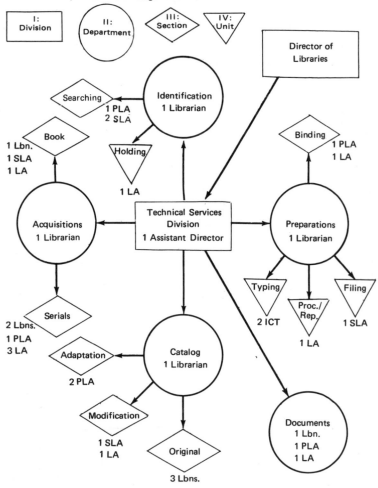

reviewed with an agent, who is selected on the basis of interest and past performance.

Budgets

The next serious consideration in the preliminary planning stage is the budget allocation. The amount of money required to underwrite this type of program for a fiscal year must be determined precisely. Attempting to predict next year's volume of publishing is difficult at best. The data based upon the past year's experience, however, are all we can use with any degree of reliability. The number of titles, the average costs, and amount of increase for both categories, therefore, all are included in the final budget figures.

Receipt of Shipments

After completing the agreement with the agent, we can expect to receive materials regularly. Shipments arrive weekly by motor freight from the agent's regional branch at Denver. The boxes are sent from the central receiving unit of the university to the library's shipping and receiving section each Wednesday. The shipment is forwarded on Thursdays at 8:00 A.M. to the acquisition department where the books are unpacked and arranged on shelves according to the LC classification noted on the packet. Areas included are humanities, social sciences, physical science, forestry and agriculture, business and economics, biomedical sciences, engineering sciences, and reference and bibliography.

Review

To allow time for faculty and librarians to examine the titles, the books remain on these shelves for one week. A schedule is posted indicating that at 2:00 P.M. the following Wednesday, the materials are to be removed—and we seldom waver from this rule. If a professor wishes to recommend retention of a title, he so indicates on a flag which is provided (see Figure 2).

The subject librarian reviews all selections title-by-title in his discipline and approves or disapproves each recommendation. He removes the books that he rejects to a separate shelf, ultimately to be returned to the agent.

Removal

Up to this point, the shipping and receiving section or the subject librarians in the public services division have been the principals involved in the internal handling of approval materials. On each Wednesday afternoon, however, the flow of the system reverts to the direction of technical services personnel.

Primary responsibility for initiating the next steps of processing rests with the identification department. First, an assistant rearranges all previously examined titles and removes them from the examination shelves to a temporary holding area according to accession number (see Figure 3). Another assistant follows this procedure by pulling the packet from each book in the shipment and realphabetizing the slips according to title entry.

Search: Phase I

An assistant begins the search process by checking the slips against the entries in the title section of the card catalog. If

FIGURE 2

```
RECOMMENDED BY


Name:


    _____


Department:


    _____







              TS:7(71)
```

FIGURE 3

____ Added Vol

____ Added Copy

____ Replacement

____ LC Copy Attached

____ NUC Copy Attached

____ LC-NUC Other Ed.

____ No Copy Found

____ Rush

____ Reserve

____ Recat: Get Other
Copy or Volume

____ Pull Cards

____ Different Edition in
Library—Call No:

____ Subject Copy
Attached

____ Author Verification
Attached

____ Curr. Awareness
Coll.

____ Restricted

____ Western

____ Special

____ Imag. Wars

____ Covers

____ Repair:
____ Spine
____ Errata
____ Paste Plates

____ Reference

____ Sci. Ref.

____ Autographed Copy

____ Noncirculating

TS:5(71)

the card is not found, a single slash mark is placed under the title. If the exact title is located, but it is:

1. a different author—a single slash is added;
2. the same author and date—a double slash is added and/or a call number;
3. the same author and different date—a double slash added and call number and edition/date;
4. a different volume—a double slash added and call number;
5. *on order* or *in process* information is added.

Search: Phase II

Next, all packets are returned by these assistants (mostly students or hourly employees) to the identification clerk. The packets are reexamined for titles in series. If so identified, a check is made against the library's holdings as listed in the *Serials Book Catalog* (a locally computer-generated product) and in the Kardex files of the serials section. If found to be on standing order, the book is immediately retrieved from the temporary holding shelf and sent, together with the packet, to the serials librarian for processing.

Search: Phase III

If the serial is not located in these sources, the new serials title catalog and the Library of Congress catalogs are consulted. If LC serial copy is found, it is sent to the serials section for processing. If it is not located, it is sent, together with a flag marked "RETURN TO HOLDINGS."

Search: Phase IV

All titles initially identified by an assistant as duplicates are rechecked by a clerk against the entries in the title section of the card catalog. Reprints are considered duplicates in this instance and automatically rejected. Upon confirming the duplication, the approval packet is rematched with the title on the temporary hold shelves, and, together, they are removed and transferred to the reject shelves.

Search: Phase V

For all added volumes, added copies, and different editions, the packets are reviewed carefully by the identification clerk and compared with the entries in the shelflist and the orders-outfiles. The goldenrod flag is marked with instructions as is the appropriate box on the approval packet slips. The call number is also added to the flag and subsequently placed in the book. Added volumes and added copies are taken directly to the modification section after the packet has been typed. Different editions, on the other hand, are processed as new titles.

Search: Phase VI

All remaining packets are forwarded at this point from the identification clerk to the book section of the acquisitions department. A typist subsequently adds to the packet: (a) initials of the librarian who approved the purchase; (b) fund code number; (c) date of receipt; and (d) intended location (if other than the general stacks). The typist next separates the slips from the packet assembly and forwards them as follows: (1) green slips to the preparations department for filing in the title card catalog; (2) white slips to the accounting section to be sent ultimately with requests for payment;

(3) yellow and remaining slips to the identification department unless the title was established as an added volume or copy whereupon the goldenrod slips are held by acquisitions department until the book is actually added to shelflist.

Search: Phase VII

Upon return of these latter slips, the identification clerk examines the yellow ones for legibility of accession number and title particularly. The slips are next used to search for catalog information in the proofslip files. If located, the yellow search slips and the LC slips are matched. If not, the yellow slip is filed in the current proofslip cumulation. All titles with proofslips are eventually matched with the approved books being held on temporary shelves. They are next transferred to trucks. An assistant transports them to the adaptation section of the catalog department.

Search: Phase VIII

Books without proofslips are matched with remaining slips in the packet, gathered from the temporary shelves, and forwarded to the holding section. These titles are held pending arrival of proofslips, but no longer than six months. At that point, a repeated search for NUC or LC copy is made for each title. If located, the items are handled as previously described and forwarded for cataloging. If not located, however, subject copy is sought and attempts to verify the author are made through routine bibliographic searches. The book is then forwarded, together with whatever information is found, to the original section of the catalog department.

Notification

Although cataloging, preparation, and storage of these approval titles are not within the purview of this report, we should mention notification to the selector of availability. This part of the process is initiated by the preparations clerk who forwards the packet slip to the subject librarian, who then notifies the faculty member when appropriate.

A description of the internal system for handling approval materials should include a few more facts. An important point to emphasize is that only one full-time clerk in the technical services complement devotes the major portion of her time to handling approval materials. It should also be stated that no calculated top priorities exist within this total system of processing.

THE FINDINGS

One purpose of the investigation was to find an internal system for handling approval plans that was operating efficiently as determined by three criteria: time, cost, and quality. As a basis for analyzing these factors, several related findings should be reviewed.

Receipts

During the calendar year 1970, 15,702 titles were received by CSU on approval from our major supplier (see Table 1). It should be noted that receipts from January through June included reprints, a practice that was discontinued during the current fiscal year. The monthly volume of titles received

TABLE 1 APPROVAL TITLES RECEIVED, RETAINED, AND RE-JECTED AT CSU, JANUARY-DECEMBER 1970

Period	Receipts	Retention	Percentage	Rejection	Percentage
January	1,830	1,414	77.9	416	22.1
February	1,179	1,014	86.9	165	13.1
March	1,270	1,058	83.1	212	16.9
April	2,201	1,945	88.9	256	11.1
May	1,315	1,153	87.6	162	12.4
June	1,259	1,140	90.4	119	9.6
Subtotal	9,054	7,724	88.4	1,330	14.6
July	1,033	942	91.2	91	8.8
August	1,085	995	91.2	90	8.3
September	1,010	934	92.5	76	7.5
October	1,198	1,106	92.3	92	7.7
November	855	814	98.2	41	4.8
December	1,467	1,366	93.9	101	6.1
Subtotal	6,648[a]	6,157	92.7	491	7.3
Grand Total	15,702	13,881	88.1	1,821	11.9

[a]Excludes reprints after July

ranges from 2,201 (14 percent) in April to 855 (5.4 percent) in November. The number of titles received during the period when reprints were sent is 9,054 (57.6 percent) as compared to 6,648 (43.4 percent) titles received from July through December 1970.

Retentions

As can be observed further in Table 1, 13,881 titles were retained, or 88.1 percent of the total received. It is noteworthy that the retention rate increased from 85.4 percent to 92.7 percent after reprints were dropped from the profile. The total number of titles retained, on the other hand, decreased from 7,724 to 6,157.

Rejections

Table 1 shows that 1,821 (11.9 percent) of the titles received were rejected and returned to the supplier. The volume of rejection ranged from 416 (22.1 percent) in January to 42 (4.8 percent) in November. As the rate of retention rose to 92.7 percent during the period when reprints were no longer sent, the rate of rejection fell correspondingly to 7.3 percent. Compared another way, the rate of rejection was cut in half from 14.6 percent to 7.3 percent.

Whereas retention is based primarily upon the evaluation of a librarian who examines the book for appropriateness to the collection, the causes for rejection include additional factors. They involve the discovery of duplication or the identification of a title as a serial rather than a monograph.

Of the total rejections during 1970 of 1,821 titles, 1,070 (58 percent) were judged inappropriate by the subject librarians (see Table 2). It was discovered that 194 (11 percent) titles were monograph duplicates and 511 (28 percent) were reprint duplicates. The remaining 46 (3 percent) were defined as serials titles and not retained for various reasons.

Another computation shows that, of all the titles received during this period (15,702), the 1,070 rejected on the basis of no value to the collection amount to only 6.8 percent (see Table 2). It is also noted that 4.4 percent of the titles received were rejected because they were duplicates (605). A mere 0.002 percent, or forty-six titles, were returned to the

TABLE 2 APPROVAL TITLES REJECTED AT CSU, JANUARY-
DECEMBER 1970

Reason	Number	Percentage
Inappropriate	1,070	58
Duplicate (monograph)	194	11
Duplicate (reprint)	511	28
Serials title	46	3
Total	1,821	100

vendor because they were classified as serials, and, therefore, beyond the profile.

Holdings

An analysis of the titles being held for catalog information was recently completed and indicated several facts. As of January 28, 1971, among the approval books retained from July through December 1970, 1,361 titles were still un-processed and held pending receipt of LC proofslips (see Table 3).

The success/failure ratio ranged from 90/10 for the titles from the August shipment to 60/40 of the materials from December receipts. The average for this post receipt period showed thus that about 22 percent of the titles lacked catalog information.

TABLE 3 APPROVAL TITLES HELD FOR LC PROOFSLIPS AT CSU, JULY-DECEMBER 1970

Period	Titles Retained	Titles Remaining	Success/Failure Ratio[a]
July	942	179	80/20
August	995	117	90/10
September	934	161	83/17
October	1,106	154	83/17
November	814	199	76/24
December	1,366	552	60/40
Total	6,157	1,362	78/22

[a] As of January 28, 1971.

Costs

To determine the cost involved in searching, 219 titles were selected at random from shipments during January 1971. The total time spent by student assistants checking the title section of the card catalog for this batch was 2 hours and 50 minutes (see Table 4). The mean time was 46 seconds, at an average cost of 2 cents.

The rechecking of each title by an identification clerk involved several steps amounting to 4 hours and 45 minutes, or an arithmetic mean per title of 1 minute and 18 seconds. The average cost for this segment of the phase based upon hourly wages was 4.5 cents.

TABLE 4 COST STUDY OF THE SEARCHING PHASE OF PROCESSING 219 APPROVAL TITLES AT CSU, JANUARY 1971

Activity	Employee	Time Required	Total Time Requirement	Mean Time	Mean Cost
Title catalog checking	Student	—	2 hrs. 50 min.	46 sec.	$0.02
SBC Checking	Clerk	55 min.			—
Kardex and card catalog	Clerk	3 hrs. 15 min.			—
Flagging and handling	Clerk	35 min.			
			4 hrs. 45 min.	1 min. 18 sec.	0.045
Filing and searching	Student		8 hrs. 00 min.	2 min. 11 sec.	0.06
Totals			15 hrs. 35 min.	4 min. 26 sec.	$0.125

The breakdown of these bits of processing includes 55 minutes in searching the *Serials Book Catalog*, 3 hours and 15 minutes in searching the Kardex files and in rechecking the title catalog, and 35 minutes in flagging books, removing rejects from temporary shelves, and other miscellaneous steps already described, yielding the previously cited total of 4 hours and 45 minutes.

The effort to search the proofslip file and to file the unmatched proofslips was handled by student assistants. This unit of processing also includes such tasks as rearranging the approval packets by accession number and transferring books from temporary to holding areas. This activity required 8 hours at a mean time per title of 2 minutes and 11 seconds. The average cost per item was 6 cents.

The total average time spent on each title in this sample of 219 items was 4 minutes and 26 seconds. Combining both types of assistance involved in the search process, one notices then that the total average cost expended for this activity is 12.5 cents per title.

SUMMARY AND CONCLUSIONS

The purpose of this study was to gather and examine data on the relationships between the various components of an internal system for handling approval materials and the effectiveness of the operation. The method followed was a series of observations and interviews in a land-grant university library. All of the responses were tabulated, structured, and presented.

Findings

The findings of the study are as follows:

1. A substantial effort is made by the library to acquire current scholarly domestic imprints, exceeding 15,000 titles in a given year.
2. A high incidence of retention is seen in the approval of nearly 90 percent of all titles received.
3. The rejection rate is explained by the fact that only about 60 percent of the disapproved titles are judged inappropriate to the collection, whereas the remainder are either duplicates or serials titles.
4. The success/failure ratio of receiving catalog information is nearly 50/50 during the first month after receipt, increasing to nearly 90/10 after six months have passed. Titles remaining without LC copy after this point amounted to 22 percent.
5. The searching and identification phase of this system suggests that the average time involved is 4 minutes and 20 seconds, at a cost of 12.5 cents.

Limitations

Conclusions and generalizations based on these findings should be drawn only after limitations and assumptions implicit in the method have been made explicit. Those relevant to this report follow:

1. The findings would be applicable to the handling of approval materials at other types of libraries only to the extent that their situations are similar to those of the library at Colorado State University.
2. The approval system was studied at a medium-size university. Technical services at small or very large academic libraries were not considered.
3. The experience with only one approval agent was studied.

The applicability to other agents cannot be made with certainty.

4. An attempt to select randomly titles for the time and cost studies was unfailing. A larger number of cases, nonetheless, might have strengthened the results.

Conclusions

Based upon the findings in the investigation and within the limitations of the study, several conclusions are drawn:

1. This university library's effort to acquire current scholarly domestic imprints is effective. The amount and variety of material obtained by the profile method of selection would more than likely be less without this arrangement.
2. The automatic receipt of current titles on an approval plan suggests a lower unit cost for ordering than the more common methods of selecting titles individually and placing firm orders.
3. With material received in close proximity to the publication date, the time span between receipt and availability to users is reduced.
4. Although there are delays while awaiting centrally prepared cataloging information, the locating of nearly 50 percent of titles upon receipt of approval items and an additional 30 percent during the next five months is significant.

Implications

There are practical implications for libraries which can be inferred from the findings and conclusions of this report.

1. As a partial answer to the shortage of materials in academic libraries, an approval plan should be considered as one means of receiving regularly and automatically a large proportion of the publishing output of current domestic scholarly imprints.
2. In allocating substantial amounts of the book budget to ensure full implementation of an approval plan, this fixed cost must be weighed against the price for the purchase of other types of important material.
3. The complexity of the process involved in operating an approval plan is related to the staff complement. There is every reason to think that once the selection phase has been achieved, however, the implementation can be handled almost exclusively by nonprofessional personnel.
4. An ongoing evaluation procedure should be developed. As systems are altered, the effectiveness of the plan may change, too. The persons responsible for this operation should be privy to future plans regarding collection development.
5. Preliminary impressions show that faculty and students appreciate the effort to acquire current domestic scholarly imprints as quickly as possible. One can infer from this response that the patron's need for current monographs is being met with reasonable satisfaction.

Future Research

Inasmuch as this study is a small-scale investigation of only one system of handling approval materials, it should be considered exploratory and preliminary. In order for the findings and conclusions to be accepted with greater confidence, other similar investigations might be undertaken.

Certain refinements in future studies are needed. Staffs

change in their behavior and attitudes. Modifications in financial support also occur from one fiscal period to another. It may be that the investigation should be conducted for more than one year.

The study could also be broadened to include other libraries. One can readily conceive developing the investigation at an institution similar to Colorado State University. The same kind of study in a large library with a vast collection could produce quite different results.

It may be of interest to determine the attitudes of patrons about the features of an approval plan. Why do some faculty members unfailingly examine materials every week? Is it their appreciation of the need to have appropriate materials in the collection, or do other factors force them into a particular behavior pattern?

Carefully controlled investigations using different methods of educating the faculty about their responsibilities could be conducted. The consideration of relevant research and other disciplines, such as behavior psychology, may have application. Motivation research has introduced new techniques, which could be applied in this area.

Broader cost studies would also be important from a management viewpoint. The successful operation of acquisitions programs in academic libraries is necessarily related to the cost. If acquiring materials is of low cost, then the program is more likely to be justified and continued. If the practice of involving faculty and librarians in the selection process is prohibitively expensive, on the other hand, it may not be feasible no matter how favorable the results are.

There is a need, finally, for continuing research into the characteristics of internal systems for handling approval materials. Although there have been some positive results from this study, many of the components of the system are still unknown and unarticulated. Progressive and precise research into the future is certainly one requisite toward understanding the library's role in bringing current resources to its users.

6

Review of
Approval Plan Methods

Harriet K. Rebuldela

This paper is not concerned with the pros and cons of approval plans, but rather with the review and selection of an appropriate plan from those available. The discussion will be limited to the examination of the three major plans that offer broad coverage of domestic English-language titles of interest to academic libraries. They are Baker and Taylor's University and College New Books Service, Bro-Dart's Books Coming Into Print Program, and Richard Abel's Approval Plan. Similarities and differences will be pointed out, but qualitative evaluation will not be made. This paper will also discuss some of the factors that must be considered in the selection of a plan.

The initiation of an approval program is not to be taken lightly. It will be a new way of life which will bring forth changes in library operations, and possibly reassignments of positions, restructuring of departments and responsibilities, and restructuring of files and their maintenance. From the outset, the plan must be accepted. Any program, no matter how sophisticated the model, cannot succeed if it encounters a hostile climate. Although the new program may become the major acquisition method, it must coexist with the other procurement methods which are retained, and librarians must not abdicate their responsibilities of book selection. The aims of the three plans are basically alike: to select, gather, and supply on approval current imprints according to the parameters set by the library. Initially then, the library must define its profile by indicating the scope and depth of the subject areas it would like the dealer to handle.

COVERAGE

The three companies have subject outlines from which the library draws its requirements. The outlines differ in specificity. Specificity is important for special libraries and libraries with a limited budget for an approval plan in certain subject areas only; but it is not so crucial for the library with a healthy budget for an extensive plan. When approval plans first appeared on the library scene, a directive commonly made by dealers and acquisition librarians was to keep the profile broad without too many restrictions. It was thought that books in marginal areas would be missed. It was also thought that *only* libraries with fair-sized budgets could take advantage of such a plan. Today, experience and refinements in the plans have made it possible for libraries with smaller budgets to have a limited approval plan.

Baker and Taylor's outline is based on broad LC classification numbers and subject headings. Some of the subjects are broken down further. Bro-Dart's subject thesaurus is accompanied by three secondary modifiers. The secondary modifiers by subject, geography, and form when applied to the basic subject outline permit a more detailed profile. Abel's subject outline allows a very detailed subject analysis. It is accompanied by what the firm calls its "nonsubject parameters," which permit a library to indicate different directives for the different subject areas for a more precise profile.

The basic subjects are covered by all three companies. Any one of the outlines will suffice if the library can state clearly what types of books it would like to receive on approval. If profiling is properly done and the expectations of the program clearly understood, administering the plan will be much simpler.

The three companies require a decision on price limitations, levels of difficulty, paperback editions, policy on reprints, and whether multiple order forms only should be supplied for books not sent on approval but which may be of potential interest. These forms for books should be used to supplement the library's title-by-title buying program. Abel, Bro-Dart, and Baker and Taylor can profile a library for forms only; no books are sent at first.

Listings of the publishers covered by the three plans are provided by the companies. These are not complete listings of all the publishers handled, but they serve an important function in ascertaining reasonably what titles might be expected. All three companies work from advanced publishers' blurbs and catalogs, review media, and LC depository cards or proofs. Upon request, Abel will provide annotated copies of *Publishers Weekly* and *British National Bibliography* that show the books they have handled on approval. The subject librarian or faculty member may review for purchase those titles not furnished on the plan.

A significant omission from the circulated lists are publications emanating from various departments of universities, art museums and galleries, and learned societies. The library desiring these types of publications should inquire whether they are available, and should state its needs, for this group of publications is often troublesome to obtain.

Presently Baker and Taylor offers United States publications and titles from Canadian university presses and the major publishers in the United Kingdom. Bro-Dart offers titles from United States publishers and other English-language publishers with distributors in the United States. Abel offers both English and foreign titles, regardless of country, in accordance with its publisher listing.

One of the papers presented at last year's seminar on gathering plans expressed the problem of not knowing what titles would actually be supplied. Although it is impossible to predict with accuracy what titles will actually be sent, the library should count on receiving a satisfactory percentage of expected books. If it does not, the plan is not effective, and the library must either revise its profile or pressure the vendor to deliver in accordance with the established profile. Libraries that feel uneasy about the inability to predict with some degree of confidence what titles will actually arrive might find the answer in Bro-Dart's advance notification cards, which may be used as an on-order document. The advance notification cards may be returned to stop shipment of titles the library does not want or to request that additional copies be supplied. After reliability of coverage is established, the library ought to reconsider the necessity of filing the advance notification cards. Filing is a costly operation. Librarians are notorious for continuing tasks no longer needed, often forgetting why the task was undertaken in the first place.

CATALOGING SERVICES

Cataloging services are offered by the three companies. Each depends on the availability of LC copy. If LC copy is available when books are shipped, Bro-Dart can provide unfinished photo-offset cards for thirty-five cents a set, two sets for fifty cents. A set consists of 3 sat. Custom-finished cards and original cataloging are available on a contract basis through their cataloging services, Alanar. Books handled through Alanar would be completely processed but cannot be sent on approval. Through Alanar, Bro-Dart can hold books to await the appearance of LC copy for, say, ninety to one hundred twenty days, before the books are processed for original cataloging. Bro-Dart receives depository cards from the Library of Congress.

Baker and Taylor is able to supply computer-produced catalog cards at fifteen cents a set and offers some format options from which a library may select. The cards may be headed and numbered, headed and unnumbered, unnumbered and unheaded. Only LC classification is offered. Books lacking LC catalog cards at the time the books are shipped are sent ahead, and the company provides cards later as they become available. Books shipped with cards are returnable. Baker and Taylor receives the first set after depository cards and MARC tapes.

Richard Abel responds to the many different cataloging demands of libraries by offering many options from which a library may structure its requirements. Both Dewey and LC classification schemes with varied stacking of call-number formats and added entries in addition to those made by LC are offered. The computer-produced cards are available for eighty cents a card set. Books and cards may be returned for full credit. Books lacking cards are shipped with cards following later as they become available. Processing kits consisting of catalog cards, labels, pocket, and circulation cards are available on a firm order basis, and retrospective LC catalog cards are also available. Abel receives both MARC tapes and depository cards.

Some books take months to get cataloged by the Library of Congress, while others never get cataloged, so it is advisable for libraries requesting catalog cards to instruct the dealer to cancel cards after a certain time period, depending upon the libraries' policy of releasing books for original cataloging. Libraries with an inadequate cataloging staff and a growing backlog of books to be processed should seriously consider utilizing the cataloging services. If local cataloging practices do not correspond with the options offered, a reexamination of current policies might be in order to determine what is really essential and what is not. Commercial firms can often provide catalog cards much faster and cheaper than some libraries can produce locally. However, before a step is taken in this direction, a library should conscientiously do a cost study to determine which method is more beneficial.

The examination of cataloging aids should not be limited to only those offered by the approval dealers. Today there are several organizations and commercial firms offering services in the area of catalog card reproduction that merit attention. They are Information Dynamic's Micrographic Catalog Retrieval System, Information Design's Cardset System, and the Ohio College Library Center System. The data base of the latter two consists of only those LC entries available on MARC tapes; however, if a large portion of books received against a library's given profile includes entries available on MARC tapes, a look at those systems might prove worthwhile. Decision to use commercial cataloging services need not be made at the time the approval plan is instituted. The needed data can first be collected and decisions made later.

CONTINUATION ORDERS

Most libraries with moderate-size budgets usually have standing orders for certain annuals, monographic titles belonging to series, and irregularly published handbooks, directories, and the like, which do not fall into the category of subscription periodicals and journals, but which the library has set up on a continuing basis. In this area, a library can confront some sticky problems should it fail to understand the limits of the dealer's capabilities and should it fail to clearly instruct the dealer what the library wants. Interfacing the existing standing orders with an approval plan can be tricky. Libraries with a serials book catalog face a unique problem. The recording and updating of continuations received on approval must be made. The decision to place certain titles on a firm standing-order basis needs to be related to the dealer. The cancellation of the existing standing order and the transfer of the standing order to the approval dealer should be seriously considered. While it is true that the simultaneous actions might produce duplicates, the long-range benefits might be quite substantial, especially in the case of monographic series that continually need to have local records made for internal handling.

Abel uses the following scheme for continuations. Continuation titles (be it volume one or a volume in progress) which fall into the subject specification are sent on approval.

Upon the receipt of the particular volume, the library may accept volumes as it wishes on a title-by-title basis, may request a standing order for all future volumes, or may ask Abel to stop shipment of all subsequent volumes of the series and provide forms only. Abel maintains a master file on the continuation orders, which it supplies to the different libraries. Upon request, Abel can provide the library with a computer-produced listing of all the continuation orders that a library has with the company, and a listing of the titles the library has asked Abel not to supply. The list cites such information as the first volume supplied, the latest volume shipped, the date the latest volume was shipped, and the library's purchase order number.

Recently Baker and Taylor has made it possible for libraries to receive titles belonging to a series in progress with the option to receive or not receive subsequent volumes in accordance with the profile and specifications.

With Bro-Dart, the library can handle series in two ways. The library may provide the company with a list of titles it would like supplied, or may request that advance notification cards be supplied for books falling into this category.

LAG TIME

Most librarians who support approval plans contend that books reach the library faster than titles ordered on a title-by-title basis, yet complaints about lag time are not uncommon. The glaring exceptions when titles expected on approval were not received by the library are related. The many times requests have been located in the library tend to get forgotten because these instances are less dramatic. I find the desire for excellence in vendor performance commendable, but I wonder if the complaints are very serious. Many users become aware of a new title through current awareness media, such as book reviews, which often appear several months after publication. Few reviews are done through galley proofs. While large libraries may have computer-created listings of the order file, and while others may file a copy of the orders in the public catalog, in most libraries, listings of uncataloged titles are not easily accessible or well known to the users, and the books sit in technical services awaiting cataloging.

It is difficult to imagine that any of the dealers under discussion is unable to get a substantial portion of the total volumes supplied to the library shortly after publication date. The very existence of the competitive firms should assure the librarians that the dealers will continually strive to reduce lag time. If we are really concerned abut lag times, we should devise effective means to make titles awaiting cataloging available to the users. Daniel Gore has suggested one way it may be done.

MIDWEST LIBRARY SERVICE

Until now, the discussion has dealt with the examination of the features of the three approval plans that gather, select, and supply books in accordance with the library's requirements. Libraries still uneasy and not convinced that approval plans suit their needs, and still preferring to select titles on a title-by-title basis through the use of proofs, might be interested in the Midwest Library Service located in Maryland Heights, Missouri. The program is named College and University Library New Books Selection and Catalog Card Service. Its coverage is limited to United States titles that are commercially procurable. Midwest receives the first set after depository cards. Pamphlets, foreign titles, and items not appropriate for academic libraries are sorted out, and the remaining universe of proof makes up the base from which the library receives copies of the proofs matching its requirements.

The company sends the library copies of proofs in the categories specified by the library. The library returns the proofs of the titles it wishes the company to obtain and may request that unit card sets be supplied. Call numbers may be typed before the orders are placed to save typing them on each unit card later. The offset printed cards may be obtained for thirty-five cents a card set (a card set comprising a minimum of eight cards). The books and cards are sent on approval and may be returned for credit.

PREBOUND PAPERBACKS

The four companies mentioned thus far will, upon request, supply prebound paperback titles. None permits returns. This is understandable. Furthermore, if the number of returns in this category is low, it might be more economical to absorb the cost of the item and to dispose of the book as the library sees fit, rather than creating costly, elaborate procedures to handle the returns. On the other hand, if many titles fall into this category, the policy of having paperback editions prebound should be reexamined.

SUMMARY

For the most part, this discussion has dealt with the features of three approval plans offering current English-language titles. Taking these features into consideration, is it possible to say which is more efficient for the different types of academic libraries? It is not. The many variables that must be taken into account make it impossible to categorize the different types of libraries and the plan that suits each best. Actually, the clue does not rest in the type library involved, but rather what the library wants the particular approval plan to do.

For the library that wants titles from the major United States trade publishers and university presses and is not concerned so much about capturing titles from societies, university departments, and minor publishers, any of the three jobbers should be able to do the job. A plan of this nature will yield a large percentage of United States titles of interest to academic libraries. I would guess that as much as 75 percent of these titles are published by as few as four hundred publishers, and that college libraries may find such a plan entirely adequate. Coverage being equal, the library must then consider which plan is easiest to handle and which offers the best service and discount.

Research libraries will find a limited plan inadequate for their needs. They will expect the dealer to gather a larger universe of books for them, a universe which includes publications from learned societies, associations, departments of universities, and museums. These are publications that often do not appear in review media and are difficult to obtain unless the titles belong to a series for which the library has a standing order. Knowledge of this group of publishers and their publishing habits requires competent, experienced bookmen, and the company that can provide the largest body of these types of materials should be selected.

Extensive and special-subject approval plans are not for

everyone. It is not for the library that must commit a large portion of its budget to meet curriculum and faculty demands. A limited-approval plan of university presses may suffice, depending on the library's inclinations. Or, if only a handful of select publishers is desired, a blanket order directly with the publisher might be advisable. By publisher blanket order, I mean an arrangement made with the publisher whereby all its publications are supplied. Publisher blanket orders do not provide multiform records for the library's use; however, discounts and delivery times are better. Blanket orders tend to increase in number with time. The growth should be monitored. When it reaches a certain size, the library should consider switching to an approval plan to take advantage of the multiforms that approval plans provide. Clerical tasks will be reduced.

English-language approval plans take care of only part of the needs of academic libraries. Research demands more in the area of foreign titles and special types of publications such as music scores, Slavic and Hebrew books, and art catalogs. These are items that are usually not easy to handle. Fortunately there are dealers specializing in supplying titles from foreign countries and special type publications. Dealers in foreign titles tend to specialize by country.

Earlier presentations have touched on the problems of capturing books not furnished on approval. The assumption here is that "core titles" are easy to obtain. Yes, they are, but the problem rests *not* in the obtaining of these books but rather in the identification of these titles. An approval plan is an act of faith in the hope of gaining efficiency. The gain will be lost if checking and rechecking is performed continuously. Even specific ordering does not bring every needed title into the collections.

7
European Discounts

Knut Dorn

The topic of discount has long been taboo in the case of every European bookdealer—and to relate it to an approval plan only makes matters worse. It is quite inconceivable when applied to books supplied on approval from European countries.

First, a word in general regarding discount practice in Germany. As everyone in the audience knows, Harrassowitz does not grant discounts and, as a matter of course, one should not expect to obtain discount from any German or European dealer, if that dealer is to maintain an established level of service in traditional book supply, let alone in serving an approval order. This is strictly in accord with the legal setup in Germany today, which stipulates that we, as book-dealers, supply to individual readers and libraries alike any book published in Germany at the publisher's catalog price. This is exactly the policy at Harrassowitz: supply at the publisher's price with no handling, no insurance, and no postage charges. When a book is ordered, the library is charged at the catalog price, which can easily be verified from the publisher's announcement and the national bibliographies; the amount is converted into American currency at the daily exchange rate.

Germany still maintains a fixed retail price agreement for books, which means that the publisher's catalog price is legally enforced. There are, of course, always those outsiders who want to get a foothold in the book trade by undercutting prices, and, in such cases, once they get to hear of it, publishers can stop supplying the dealers concerned; this has actually been done in a number of cases. There is one exception to this rule, and it pertains to German scholarly libraries, which are, by law, permitted to claim a 5 percent discount once they have fulfilled certain requirements; they must have a certain number of volumes already in their possession, a current budget of a stated size, and the proof that they are furthering research and scholarly reading. This discount, however, is granted only upon the understanding of immediate payment to the local dealer, who incurs no overhead costs in the way of mailing and transporting the material to his neighboring institute or university library.

This setup is, of course, not enforced outside the boundaries of Germany, and, theoretically speaking, the German dealer exporting books to America could grant a discount without violating the legal trade agreement. In our estimation, however, he cannot do so if he is to operate in a responsible manner and see to it that his library customers receive the kind of attention that has been established in the relationship between research libraries and European international bookdealers. It is possible that a German bookdealer could grant a discount on "easy" material, but then he would either have to raise the price charged for the remainder—the rare, out-of-the-ordinary publications, the material from private presses and from outside the regular trade, all of which may take innumerable pains to procure—or else he would have to refuse to provide such books at all. We all know, however, that the difficult material will have to be procured just the same, if the demands of a university library are to be met.

There are libraries who try to get the best of both worlds and give the easy orders to a vendor granting discount, leaving the "cats and dogs" to firms such as Harrassowitz. This, we feel, is a most unfair procedure and could put us out of business in time. It is unfair not only to us, but also to the other research libraries in the country, which, in a manner of speaking, have to cofinance the acquisition program of their "clever" colleagues. We know, for example, that out of any five titles which we supply, only three will give us a reasonable margin of profit. To supply a book below the price of six dollars is in itself a loss, no matter what the discount granted us. We can only hope that with the support of libraries we will be able to keep an acceptable balance of business.

The discount structure in German publishing is no secret; on scholarly books, it ranges from 20 to 30 percent passed on from publisher to bookdealer. Sometimes there is a 35 percent, and, very rarely, a 40 percent discount, which is the point at which attractive business starts. Our overheads amount to 28.9 percent, mainly due to the large salaries expected by a professional staff. This means that a less than 30 percent discount does not allow us to break even, and, believe me, there are many such transactions. Fiction and belles lettres offer the most favorable discount, going up to 45 percent, but, as you know, only a small volume of our business comprises this type of publication.

In other words, if a German bookdealer working within this setup starts giving discounts, he risks his own chances of remaining in business, or he has to increase prices in advance, or again, he must decide to deal exclusively in so-called attractive material. There is really no other way unless—and this has been heard of before—he simply finances his library service from other branches and activities of his company.

The handling charge has been discussed in connection with the European approval plans. When Harrassowitz began to carry the Farmington Plan assignments and early blanket orders, we decided to stick to our old policy. We continued to do so when the more intricate approval-plan service was developed. It meant book evaluation and selection on an individual basis for each participating library, precataloging and typing of entries on any kind of form the library may have suggested, the overall return privilege, the credit service, the printing of multiple forms, and, above all, the many internal checking procedures involving new titles, plus any separate orders which the library may have decided to place—this with a view to avoiding duplication. And those are only the more obvious and costly aspects of an approval order arrangement. So far, we have tried, successfully, to maintain our "no discount, no handling charge" policy and shall make every effort to continue doing so for as long as possible. We shall continue to offer our approval plan on the same price policy as we do any of the specific orders which libraries place with us.

It is, of course, much easier and less time-consuming and costly, though also less challenging, to procure a book for which a library has specifically asked. The approval plan, on the other hand, has attractions of which we are well aware and which we do not value lightly. The dealer entrusted with an approval plan has, to a certain extent, an exclusive brief for current publications in his area. In its own interests, the library will help avoid duplication if it places continuations and book orders beyond the bookdealer's selection, solely with him, so giving him the chance to check his own approval files. This attraction alone should, we think, keep the dealer from adding a handling charge to his approval service. We have not done so thus far, and shall, at least for as long as present circumstances prevail, continue our policy of no discount and no handling charge. This may, however, cause us problems from another angle. I remember the spontaneous remark of a librarian who, on principle, would not join our approval plan accounts, but inquired into the details of our arrangements. He said: "Well, Mr. Dorn, if you provide all that service to the approval-plan participants, then you should give a discount to those of us who place all their German orders with you in the traditional way, spelling out each title required."

The only answer here is: "Rather than, or instead of a discount, why not avail yourself of the advantages of entering into an approval plan with Otto Harrassowitz?"

8
Dealers' Panel[1]

Moderator: Hugh C. Atkinson

ATKINSON: We have with us this morning Dean Spain, chairman of the board of Baker and Taylor; Jack Walsdorf, library services adviser to Blackwell's; Knut Dorn, head of the export division of Harrassowitz; Tom Martin, vice president of East Coast operations of Richard Abel Company; Nelson Bennion, sales manager of Books Coming into Print division of Bro-Dart. We have a substitution, Douglas McCleary, who is in charge of blanket order plans for music for Alexander Broude, and Mr. Broude is also here; and we have Ralph Lessing, vice president of Stechert-Hafner.

I have asked each of the panelists to speak for three to eight minutes, and Mr. Walsdorf will begin.

WALSDORF: Thank you very much, Mr. Atkinson. As Robert Wedgewood reported in the spring 1970 issue of *Library Resources and Technical Services,* writing about foreign-book dealers, some dealers responded to him that they thought the blanket order had but a meager advantage be-

1. The panel discussion has been edited.

cause it took so much more labor and time to run such a program. We at Blackwell's are in general agreement, yet we feel that it is this blanket-buying plan more and more libraries are being forced to undertake because of their own internal problems and costs. We have, therefore, devoted our best staff to the operation of blanket-order plans (by "best," I mean that this is an area where the greatest degree of skilled personnel is needed). We have also undertaken a project to create invoicing and accounting practices designed to fill the needs of individual blanket-order accounts.

Although we have had to make some adjustments in order to fill blanket orders smoothly, we have not found that it has changed our bookstock or our policies. The advent of the blanket order has simply meant that our selectors will find most of the titles they need already on our shelves. This is true because we are a scholarly bookshop. In a university bookshop of this type, we are forced by our clientele to have academic titles in stock for long periods of time after the date of publication.

For us, internally, the greatest advantage of the blanket-order plan is that our selectors will sometimes advise our buyers on titles which have not been ordered in advance of publication, but which the selector feels will be in great demand. This advance knowledge can spell the difference between getting a large order to the publisher just before the title is OP or having to report the title to a customer as out-of-stock. As a general rule, we like to feel that we send on a blanket-order book selection plan those titles a library would have ordered if they were selecting from the *British National Bibliography*. The quality of the orders handled is high no matter who selects the titles.

Having committed ourselves and our most knowledgeable

staff to blanket-order operations, we have little doubt that the future will see an increased use of this service. We hope that our staff and our stock of materials on hand, which covers the entire range of publishing, along with the complete range of service, including the handling of out-of-print searching, government publications, periodicals, sheet music, and back files, will be a deciding factor in the minds of librarians who are trying to find a dealer who will not only handle their easy items but also the difficult ones. Thank you.

ATKINSON: Mr. Knut Dorn of Harrassowitz.

DORN: When I was asked to talk about the effects of the approval plan on our organization, I thought, well, how can I do that in ten minutes—so my statement is very sketchy.

After fifteen to twenty years (the earlier approval and blanket orders have now been in effect for more than ten years, and the newer, more comprehensive operations for nearly five years), there are bound to be changes, and some are obvious.

I would like to point out, however, that these have not really been sudden changes of concept. When there are changes, they are more in the line of a refinement of services. During my talk, I'm going to mention as changes bibliographic control and the maintaining of as flexible a serivce as possible by close cooperation with librarians, though I think this has been part of our tradition even before the blanket orders and approval orders started.

Such a refinement is probably most obvious in the area of bibliographic control. Several bibliographers on our staff have as their sole function the obtaining of information by cooperating with publishers as closely as possible; this includes the receiving of prepublication announcements and checking them. I should say that the problem that was mentioned yesterday (that a dealer might miss a relevant publication in his area) doesn't for all practical purposes exist for us anymore. Bibliographic information comes at various stages from prepublication information to citation in the national bibliographies. Series A and B of the *Deutsche Bibliographie* are checked, just to make sure that no title has escaped our attention, and since some specialists are assigned to cover the underground presses, the literary avant-garde, and music scores, I think we've managed to give pretty good coverage.

This bibliographic information, including prepublication information, is shared with the German national libraries and book trade centers, and with LC. This is a two-way operation. They get the information that we have and we, in return, get the information they may have. This exchange is very valuable.

By the way, we have an arrangement with LC to the effect that any title that we select and send on one of our approval orders goes to LC within their Title II project. The understanding is that the LC card then is ready within a short period of time.

Of course, a dealer really can perform specialized service only in his own area, so to speak, and, in our case, the German-speaking and -publishing area. I certainly wouldn't dare attempt the same services covering other countries where the bookdealer on the spot has a much better chance to solve the problems.

The most obvious change in our internal operations is the correlation between departments to make sure that series and continuation departments know exactly what the approval-order people do and avoid duplication. There has been an intricate internal checking procedure following very closely the kind of searching librarians do. This procedure really helps us to give libraries the option to continue separate series and standing orders if they want to, or incorporate them into the approval plan. And I very much concur with Mr. Walsdorf from Blackwell's that it is definitely not necessary to cancel standing orders or series once you go to an approval plan. If you entrust a dealer with an approval plan, I guess you should expect from him the kind of procedures that help him not to duplicate any series which he knows to be on standing order, with his own firm or with another.

One of the main things, as I said, is to maintain a service as flexible as possible and to be able to incorporate the individual requirements of any participating library. The technical procedures, like invoicing, can be done either on multiple-part forms or individually. Here again, the library has the option.

I should say that not a single one of our customers' approval plans in North America coincides with the other one, so it really comes to selecting with the individual requirements in mind. This goes down to a very detailed level, so it's really the book that is evaluated and the contents of the book that decides whether it is going to be included. Criteria such as whether the publisher publishes more or less than five books per year don't apply.

None of the approval plans, I should say, stands now as it was originally conceived. Such plans usually are modified after certain periods of time, usually after the first six or eight months or a year, and some subject areas are left out, others are brought in, emphasized or changed. Close cooperation with the librarian is maintained, so that we do get to know about any change of emphasis in the various department, new areas to be added, different selections to be made, and here we try to share in the responsibility and come up with the necessary information. Our returns are very carefully checked and thus we have a corresponding profile for each participating library which, based on the returns, changes constantly.

ATKINSON: Mr. Dean Spain from Baker and Taylor.

SPAIN: I suppose that Baker and Taylor is one of the dealers that has the greatest growing pains in changing over from a regular wholesaler to servicing universities and colleges as they should be served not only on the approval plan, but on all of their book needs. Baker and Taylor, over the years, has been one of the leading suppliers of books of a general nature, and what we used to do was to have a new book buyer to whom the salesmen from the publishers generally came and sold new books in advance of the publication date. That covered about 75 percent of the new titles that were published. We made one check to make sure that we didn't miss any popular new titles which public libraries need immediately on publication and that was of the review media to make sure that book was on hand at the time that we needed it.

But about three years ago, we decided that the world was sort of passing us by because we weren't doing a job in the academic library area. As a result, our sales were suffering. Then, when we started to work in that area, we found out how little we did know about this whole situation. So we decided that we'd better mend our fences and get involved in service to the academic-library market. It wasn't an easy one, and it wasn't one of those things that you get for nothing. We had to start from scratch. We had to build a whole new organization. Mr. Roth came on board about that time to help us get started in that area. We had our problems. We didn't do it entirely on a hit-and-miss basis, but we did make a lot of mistakes. We started on one route and had to change and go down another road.

But the thing that was brought out was that we were lacking the staff to handle this sort of program. So we had to gather a group of professional librarians to do the work for us. None of us knew how. I don't. I'm not a librarian. We had to consult with librarians in the field as to how to go about providing adequate service. And although it had been going for a while and we did have some guidance, we still had to develop the whole system in-house.

It has been an expensive one. It continues to be more expensive than the normal method of receiving orders and fulfilling orders. I'm not prepared at this moment to tell you exactly how much more per book it costs, but it's substantially more to handle books and do a job under the approval plan than it is normally picking and packing and shipping and billing books to public libraries, school libraries, and even to university and college libraries that send orders. A lot of that cost is fixed, and, as the volume grows, that cost of the books goes down, but many costs do not.

Now, as we developed this approval plan, we found that we were lacking in other service areas. We have not had a very good reputation among university and college librarians because of such practices as incomplete shipments, and many of you in this room have been critical of our company for that very fault.

A dealer needs advance bibliographic information to do a successful job on an approval plan. We hadn't used it before; we hadn't needed it before, and we were sort of asleep at the switch.

The approval plan, though, became something of a catalyst for us, and it led us into other areas of service to university and college libraries. From that approval plan, we developed the *Current Books for Academic Libraries*. This is a monthly publication put out by Baker and Taylor. It includes every title that has been chosen under the approval plan, and we made such a decision because we felt that the smaller libraries which do not have enough budget money to participate in an approval plan at least should have access to the information. It's a free publication; we send it to anyone who wants it. If the title itself is fairly descriptive, we do nothing except list the title. If the title isn't self-descriptive, our librarian adds a brief description. Libraries use it primarily as a tool for selection of books or for keeping up with what's available.

Baker and Taylor, in the act of developing this approval plan, began to realize that the depth of our inventory wasn't enough to supply books promptly to university and college libraries. So, over the last two years, we increased out listings from about 125,000 titles to the 200,000 titles we now carry in stock. The extra 75,000 titles are practically all titles that are for use with the approval plan and are important to university and college libraries.

We know we haven't reached the final stage in services to universities and college libraries. We're trying to improve all the time. We're dedicated to the fact that we're going to do it, but we're going to need a lot of help and we ask everyone to help us as we go along. Thank you very much.

ATKINSON: Mr. Tom Martin from the Richard Abel Company.

MARTIN: Before I begin, let me correct one small error seemingly generally believed by libraries. The current policy of the Abel Company places no limit on the minimum number of books the publisher must release in the course of a year if that publisher is to be included in our approval plan. One good book is sufficient.

There's no doubt that the approval program is modified by the internal operations of the vendor. The first thing that we have had to do is establish a method for analyzing and selecting something like 175,000 anticipated titles each year. From this mass, we select approximately 25 percent, roughly 45,000 titles, in the Western languages in the hope that we will be able to purchase them in advance of publication. In the vast majority of cases we can, but ordering from a publisher never guarantees delivery, so we have an elaborate follow-up procedure. We use the national bibliographies, LC depository cards, reviews, etc., the same tools the library must use, to identify the titles that have not been received and pick up any misses from first selection. All of these decisions are placed in a central computer-maintained file and, of course, the claiming system is based on the same computer file.

When a book arrives, it passes first through a book-profiling section. Book profiles and library profiles are, of course, each developed from a common language. The common language is a subject thesaurus and a group of nonsubject terms. The possible combinations which might be applied to a particular book are something on the order of ten million. It is a very flexible system. It allows for a very, very precise statement of what a library needs and what a book is. I should emphasize, however, that there is much judgment involved. Book profile, then, is put up in computer. If a match is made with a library profile, a decision is made to send the book.

Another major task that we've had to face is the integration of standing-order records into the approval procedures. The most pressing need has been demonstrated over and over again for good serial and standing-order control in libraries, and it is a very elusive thing.

We have now a standing-order file which contains about 25,000 series titles, nonjournal titles, I should emphasize. As each book comes through the approval program, if it happens to be in a series, it's passed against that file to see whether it should be sent as a standing order or as an approval item.

Of course, the library must maintain options to order books that have not arrived on approval, so this means that, in addition to integrating standing orders as I just described, we also have to integrate our firm order processes. Somehow or other a library must have the option of initiating an order, and this must be maintained as a phase of the approval program. This means that we must be able either to answer a response, send a book on approval, or send the same book on a firm order and not ship it on approval. So, we have developed a set of files to do that.

The administration of all these activities clearly requires the caliber personnel on a professional level of competence that is beyond the traditional vendors' operation as it was ten or fifteen years ago, and we've been very fortunate on that score. We've been able to attract, and perhaps even more important, to keep, really good people, good professionals, good subject specialists, good language specialists; that is one of the happiest aspects of this job—the quality of the people who have come together to deal with this problem.

With those people, we have also been able to get out into libraries and to work with libraries very, very closely in a way that, again, has not been traditional. We are very concerned with what your problems are and where we can do things to aid in the solution of those problems. I think that practically every development in this field by this firm and other firms can be traced back to a spirit that allows for a kind of mutual perception of problems and mutual decisions on how to solve those problems. It is very much a two-way street. In that sense, it's a very fascinating business.

We hope that as time goes by, we'll be able to improve our services not only to provide broader services, but services on a much higher level of refinement.

ATKINSON: From the Bro-Dart Corporation, Mr. Nelson Bennion.

BENNION: Bro-Dart is now in its third year of trying to offer an approval program suitable for academic and university libraries. With our computer, we've come a long way. Although we still have some bugs to get out of the program, I think that now we can say that we can satisfy at least the requirements of domestic publications for university libraries.

So far, we've tried to limit our coverage to those titles published or distributed in the United States, and we also cover the Canadian university presses.

There is one thing that is a little different with our program than with any other. We attempt to let the library know exactly which titles are going to be sent to it. This is done in the form of a duplicate three-by-five card which is sent weekly to the library; it lists the author, title, series entry, proposed publication date, publisher, price, availability dates, LC number, and ISBN (if we can get it).

We don't try to make any qualitative evaluation of the title. If it's published at what is considered an academic level, it is included in the program. We feel that you librarians are in a better position to decide, and also to limit, your collection. This advance notice also specifies the subject area that we feel this book fits.

We have experienced some difficulty in obtaining sufficient and accurate information from publishers in advance of the actual publication of the book. I'm sure all of you have had experience with title changes and cancellations, and we have not found an effective way to advise the library of these changes before they actually get the book. I think we have pretty much solved the problem, however, by being sure that the entry that we show on our three-by-five copy multiple order invoice does agree with the title page of the book. If this entry is changed in any appreciable way, such as different lead author or a different first word in the title as we originally announced it, so that the library cannot locate the advanced notice card to clear their files, we will put an errata slip in the book with the invoice, telling how it was originally announced. I think that is working fairly well right now.

There is one other advantage with our advance notice cards. The library can control pretty much how heavily they collect in a given subject. If they have a budget cut, they can send back more rejections. Or, on the other hand, we can set up the plan so that we will only ship those books the library tells us to ship.

The third way that this plan operates when we know that we have a refined profile on the library, on a budget to support such a profile, is to ship without advanced notice cards. There is a problem of filing the advance notice cards, and in some libraries that can be quite a problem.

We know that with the budget cuts that are pretty general throughout the United States, librarians on approval plans are going to have to be more selective than in the past. For instance, there may be four or five physical chemistry books that you would have purchased in the past year, and you may cut that down to three. I think you ought to have a choice in advance as to which three you'd want to keep, and I think our program gives you this opportunity.

Along quite another line, I want to tell you about something we're looking into. As you know, more and more nonbook media are being used in university libraries, and we are looking into the possibility of working some kind of approval program on this type of media. We think it's quite necessary because the available bibliographic information is not adequate.

For many years now, elementary and high school libraries have been relying quite heavily on nonbook media. We think that this may be a trend also in university and college libraries.

I think that's all I'll say at this time. I'll be at one of these tables, and I'll give you an answer to any specific questions you may have about our program later this afternoon. Thank you.

ATKINSON: Many of us have had problems with specialized areas such as music, geology, and astronomy, and we have with us one representative of a specialist dealer in music. Mr. McCleary from Alexander Broude.

McCLEARY: I must confess the feeling of a very small fish in a very large pond. I represent the firm of Alexander Broude which is specifically a music publisher and music dealer located in New York. I must also confess we are a little proud of our reputation as one of the few dealers in this country who supplies not only American music, but music from all around the world.

Prior to 1961, our firm had not been involved in music approval or gathering plans. However, on the request of the New York Public Library, Music Division, we decided to involve ourselves in what we call our music gathering plan. This was specifically set up by the New York Public Library because of the particular needs they had. They found it more and more expensive to hire people who were really knowledgeable in the field of music and collecting music. So the agreement set up was that we would supply to them, from 1961 on, all new music from all over the world, with a few small exceptions, and those exceptions included books, which we were not allowed to supply, and certain small areas like Red China and Russia.

It was our problem to set up a way, since we are a very small firm, in which we could collect material and supply it to the New York Public Library. If you know the music publishing business, you are aware that there is no particular place that one can go to find out what books are being published at what time. So we were forced to go to the Library of Congress for bibliographic data, to go to each individual publisher setting up standing orders, to try to hassle with the problem of exclusive dealerships in this country, which is really a problem in a music distributing firm.

We are aware of the unique problems faced by music librarians who have been deluged by a large accumulation of catalogs and "for sale" lists, special announcements, music journals, and periodicals all waiting to be scanned, considered, and acted upon. Therefore, to help relieve this acquisitions bottleneck, we are offering a music gathering plan to a number of large libraries with the possibility of modified plans for smaller institutions. It is our desire to place our knowledge and expertise in this very specialized field at your service.

A little bit on the side: it's been our experience that, with the advent of music in cultural centers, the traveling composer as the guest speaker, the nationall televised performances of major symphony orchestras, and the composer-in-residence programs, the music of today should be available when it is needed, and particularly to the universities.

Of course, of primary concern to most university librarians, is the fact that music departments are anxious to add to their program M.A.'s in music and Ph.D.'s in musicology. These degrees require a library with up-to-date materials. Music publishing itself is in a state of flux.

In Washington, D.C., two weeks ago, the Music Library Association was given an example of the way music is changing. Ten years ago, for a violinist to bow a certain note, it was indicated in one particular way in a piece of music. Now in contemporary music, forty-five different emblems and symbols have been devised by forty-five different composers to show how they want their particular note played. As you can see, that's a real problem.

The thing to do now is to find a way for our firm to involve itself in more of these gathering plans in more libraries. We have at this time five major university and public libraries involved with our gathering plan, and we are interested in adding to this collection of libraries, which will enable us to put more time and more money into solving the problem.

Another factor to be considered is that there are very few qualified librarians in the field of music. For example, just to test your ability in the field of music, I wonder how many of you know how many different types of scores there are. For instance, are you aware there is such a thing as a full score, a performance score, a study score, a miniature score, a condensed score, a reduction, a vocal score, an octavo score, and a choral score? Very often people request a score, and we have a tremendously difficult problem of finding out what kind of score they are interested in. Therefore, we think that with our expertise and with the people who are hired by our firm (all musicians and all involved in contemporary music making and music selling), we have something to offer to all of your libraries. Thank you.

ATKINSON: And from Stechert-Hafner, Mr. Lessing.

LESSING: I once had a beautiful paper written on these unspeakable subjects. Now I have just a few notes and since I have described the activities of Stechert-Hafner before, I'll keep within generalities this time and just discuss the effect these plans have had on us.

Before I get into this, I want to answer some questions about the minimum size of an approval plan. I would say one book a year. If, for instance, the library feels the need of *a* book in the Tagalog language per year to keep their linguistic department up to date, that can be enough. So there's no minimum.

Now what effect have these gathering plans had on us? One of them is the size of our inventory, and that has been exactly the opposite from what a previous speaker has said. We found that we need less inventory because the approval plan or gathering plan, whatever you call it, has cleaned off a sort of the top of the market. Where once we needed a number of copies of a French book, now we find people who used to buy them from our shelves get them automatically. So titles and copies in inventory have diminished.

One very positive effect of the gathering plans has been the possibility it has afforded us to start new offices abroad and extend our existing offices. Before we began LACAP, there was no reason for us to maintain an office in Latin America. LACAP gave us the basis for that. There has to be a certain amount of money coming in before you can afford to open an office in Bogotá, and this was guaranteed to us at the beginning by LACAP by the initial combination of public libraries, the University of Texas, and LC. It also gives us the possibility of more people in the field looking for these books.

Certain problems have been created by this trend toward

approval plans. The largest, and the one that disturbs us the most, is returns. Now we don't have a true approval plan. We have a blanket-order plan, and a certain number of returns are inevitable. Nobody's fault, as a matter of fact. There's an honest difference of opinion whether a certain book belongs to theology or philosophy. There are borderlines, and we err sometimes; whether we're right or wrong, we take the book back. Some of those books can't be sold, and we can't turn it back to the agent down in Bogotá or Rio.

We have found, as others have, the need for more skills and educated personnel to make a real decision on subject classification. This takes a certain amount of erudition.

Now the procedures required for the implementation of these plans are, of course, more sophisticated than the previous order-filling type of procedures, and there I agree very much with Mr. Spain. Automation, and in particular, all kinds of involved forms are necessary.

There has been a need for greater bibliographic activity. With the gathering plan came the need for catalog cards to go with them, or to get coordination with LC. Cataloging in publication is almost here. A very happy condition exists when your agent is also a Title IIC agent because then we can cooperate with LC, and you know you're going to get cards for these books. The same book that we select in France, LC has already received by air.

The question of air shipment has been raised. It would be prohibitively expensive if we shipped every book separately, let's say, from Buenos Aires, but the people that have got it from LACAP have made it possible for us to ship by air freight all the Argentine books. And we're looking into further uses of air freight in other countries. This was not possible before but now we can do it.

We have benefited from these gathering plans by being better informed bibliographically, especially in the expansion of national bibliographies. We get the books. Nobody knew they existed. We didn't know they existed until they had been shipped to us. And if we didn't get the books, there would be no way for you or us to know that these books existed in many, many cases.

I have a last point, and it is a rather interesting one. We have been told by agents abroad that the fact that American libraries have entered gathering plans has stimulated publishing and has made it possible for marginal books to be published. It sounds incredible, but the fact that we could buy forty books, forty copies of a book, and that we would announce it elsewhere and therefore stimulate the book further has made it possible for certain books, in Argentina for instance, to be published. I don't know if that's good. Maybe they're trash but it's a fact and one of the effects of the gathering plans. Thank you.

9
Summary Statement

Richard E. Chapin

I confess that I wrote the summary of this meeting last Thursday, and I haven't had to change a word! Seriously, however, I thought that this would be a simple process of gathering notes and telling you what you heard. It doesn't work out quite that simply, but let me try to review with you some impressions I have of what has been discussed.

First, we don't know what we're talking about. No one has been able to define the difference between a gathering plan, an approval plan, blanket order, or other such projects that are designed to sell us more books. Gormley took a shot at it yesterday; I hope that when he gets around to final editing of his speech, he will define some of the words that we throw around so very casually. If you ask if MSU is involved in gathering plans, my answer is no. We have no standard English-language approval plan, but we do have a plan for university presses, for selected medical publishers, and for about fifty other publishers. So, do we have an English-language gathering plan? I don't know! But I do know that we need definitions so that we all are talking about the same thing.

Now let me put this conference in perspective. There are some problems connected with approval plans, and the major one is financial, especially for 1970/71 and 1971/72. I see some of our bookdealer friends here who must view with concern libraries' commitment of more and more of their funds for approval plans and more and more of their funds for subscriptions. (Fred Wagman, University of Michigan, indicated last week that over 50 percent of his materials budget is for current subscriptions; some 40 percent of the MSU book budget is for current subscriptions.) Assuming little or no increase in book funds, there will be precious little left after paying for current issues of serials and the various approval plans. Over the next two or three years, we are going to have tight library budgets. The more money we commit to approval plans, the less we have for other library development. But this is not necessarily bad. The major adjustment will be the lack of flexibility for the next two or three years.

Now let me categorize the types of approval plans about which we have been hearing: "vacuum sweeper," "efficiency," and "in lieu of talent."

The first type, what I call the "vacuum sweeper" approach, is the rationalization of the large research library that is more interested in coverage than in selection. As Gormley pointed out: "today's junk is tomorrow's gem." Lane's survey of the ARL libraries showed heavy commitment to approval plans, a position that Anderson concurred with. We had too little discussion of collection use, but the comments of Rebuldela and Anderson give me an opportunity to hypothesize on collection use, and, hopefully, to justify the vacuum-sweeper approach.

I have a theory that x percent of all research done on a

university campus is based upon materials published in the last y years. You can use any figure for x and y; I use 80 percent and ten years. If 80 percent of all research done on a campus uses materials that have been published in the last ten years, it becomes very important to have a good current acquisitions program. If the approval plans sweep in everything current, then in ten years that collection will be equal to any other for most research use.

The question is, what is the extent of current receipts? Anderson's figures suggests 15,000 titles. What is the minimum number of titles that gives us the good current collection? Rebuldela alluded to this question, but no one gave us a workable answer. But Gore, and others indirectly, all stressed the importance of current receipts, with Gore even placing a moratorium on retrospective buying.

The second type of approval plan, and the one most discussed at this conference, is the "efficiency" approach. The papers by Gormley, Axford, and Gore were concerned with how to get the books in as quickly as possible and to get them on the shelf. If there was one point of agreement among the speakers, it was that approval plans are efficient.

The efficiency approach is the rationalization of approval plans for the new libraries and newly developing libraries. These are the libraries that suddenly have a half-million dollars for book purchase, and two people in technical services. The *only way* for these libraries is to ask the dealer to give them the books, and they'll find some way to process them. Efficient processing was the core of the papers by Anderson and Rebuldela; and Gore has even designed his FASTCAT collection. It is amazing to me that the papers seem to indicate that books received on approval plans get on the shelves at hardly any cost. There is no rationalization left for staff in technical services. We may soon have a new approach to staffing libraries: one approval plan is equal to x staff in cataloging and x plus y staff in acquisitions.

The "efficiency" papers ignore two things: discounts and selection costs. There is a variation in discounts. As Rebuldela reviewed the existing approval plans, I was sorry she didn't get a discount comparison: some offer 7 percent, some offer 15 percent. And we still have selection costs, which were glossed over in favor of getting the books on the shelf. Axford spoke of efficiency, but didn't give much consideration to staff time involved in examining current receipts.

Before leaving the efficiency of approval plans, consideration should be given to the speed of receipt. Some speakers indicated that we get books faster with the efficiency approach. Anderson and Axford both mentioned this. I say "so what?" especially if the books must wait two or three months for receipt of LC copy. Speed of receipt is important only if the books are made available immediately, as in the case of Gore's FASTCAT.

My final category of approval plans is what I call the "in lieu of talent" approach. Only a few libraries can afford all of the subject and language competencies required to develop effective collections. The "in lieu of talent" approach permits any library a great diversity: language specialists (Four Continent Book Corporation for Slavic materials), subject experts (Broude for music), and geographical emphasis (Stechert-Hafner for Latin America). Most of the papers were concerned with the larger, more inclusive gathering plans, but it is, perhaps, the specialized plans that offer more for the typical library.

After one categorizes and describes the approval plans that were discussed, what else is left to say in a summary? The overall impression one gets is that approval plans are all good: Lane's survey showed that everyone was doing it; Gormley and Axford claim that if an approval plan fails, it is due to bad management; and the dealer's panel left the impression that only the best people in the book business handle approval plans, and that they can and will devise a plan to give the library whatever it wants.

There were a few allusions and some unanswered questions, however, which indicate that all is not perfect in approval-land. What can the plans do for the smaller libraries? What is the role of the dealer as the market becomes saturated? Is book selection no longer the primary activity of librarians? What is the "profile" of a library?

The registration list for this conference is quite different from the earlier ones held in Kalamazoo: the majority here are from the smaller libraries, not the larger ones. Perhaps it is geography: West Palm Beach in February is much to be preferred over Kalamazoo. But one gets the feeling that it is the smaller library that is now considering approval plans. Lane's survey showed that the larger libraries are already involved; they used this conference two years as a source for decision-making. Today's decisions are being made by smaller libraries.

What can approval plans do for the smaller libraries? Atkinson asked the dealer's panel this question, and as of now no one has answered. What is the minimum commitment a library has to make for plans to be worthwhile? If the minimum commitment is seventy-five thousand dollars, then few college libraries can afford approval plans.

No one denied that the approval plans are big business. Anderson, Gormley, Gore, and Axford all pointed to this fact. A little arithmetic shows a gross of at least $10 million, and this is just the top of the iceberg. Lane's survey pointed to the heavy commitment of ARL libraries; Axford, Anderson, and others stressed the involvement of the developing libraries. There must be a minimum of a hundred libraries in the approval plans at the $100,000 level, the minimum suggested in some papers, specifically Gormley's. This gross figure could be increased considerably by looking into the specialist plans and other libraries that are involved but not talking about it.

With such widespread involvement of libraries and commercial concerns, what is the role of the dealer, or the dealers acting in consort, in providing bibliographic aids and assuring fuller coverage? Atkinson suggested to the dealer's panel that they have an obligation to provide 100 percent, not the easy 85 percent from *Publishers Weekly*. This can best be done, so says Atkinson, by use of *CBI* and by developing new bibliographic and selection tools.

A consort of dealers working to improve the approval plans seems much to be preferred to the alternative: fierce competition in a marketplace that just may be saturated on the basis of today's operations.

Most papers presented at this conference have mentioned, however slightly, book selection. I challenge any of you to convince bona fide book selectors—the Felix Reichmanns, the Cliff Stewarts, and many others—that there is any relationship between approval plans and book selection. Anderson indicated that he received good participation by his faculty; Rebuldela indicated that approval plans did not mean no book selection; but Gore has declared a moratorium on retrospective purchasing while having current materials "sent in" rather than "selected for." Roth stole my best line by pulling from his briefcase a copy of the proceedings of last year's conference on approval plans: an item that had *not* been selected, listed, or considered for approval plans. (This in spite of the fact that the publisher, International Scholarly Book Services, is a subsidiary of Abel Company, the grandfather of approval-plan purchasing.)

It is obvious to everyone, except perhaps a few diehards, that there can be no abdication of book selection. Selection will be necessary to fill the gaps, as well as to examine and discard (return) items sent on approval. And if the selection is good, finding items not included and/or returning items received, the professional gap (similar to the generation gap) between selector and dealer widens. But if we are not the final judge of what will be added to our collection, if we abdicate the important role of book selection, then what is the nature of our work (profession)?

We have heard much about profiles at this conference. Everyone has a profile. If we define a good profile, all relevant books suddenly will appear before publication. (Do you really believe it?) Dan Gore convinced me in his paper that selection should not reflect the past. But a profile, by definition, reflects the past, or, at best, represents today. Universities change; programs change; people change; the emphasis changes. And as they change, what happens to the profile? Once you get something into the computer, it's difficult to get it out. If we are depending entirely on a profile in developing a contract with the dealers, we should plan to change our description on a weekly, or a quarterly, or a semiannual basis. An unchanging profile is impossible for collection development today.

And now we conclude the third, and hopefully the last, International Conference on Approval Plans. I wonder what else there is to confer about on approval plans. They are here;

we know they're here; we are using them. And I'd say that at this point in time, there is not much new left to be said. You run a beautiful conference, Peter, and I hope you have another one, but not on approval plans!

Appendixes

The Program

WEDNESDAY, FEBRUARY 17, 1971

P.M.

3:00- 4:00 Registration

4:00- 4:15 Welcome - Mr. Eugene A. Robinson, Special Assistant to the President, Florida Atlantic University

4:15- 5:15 Mr. David O. Lane
  Research into a Total Effect of Approval Plans on the Nation's Academic Libraries

5:15- 7:30 Dinner Hour

8:30- 11:00 Hospitality Hour - Reception

THURSDAY, FEBRUARY 18, 1971

A.M.

8:30- 9:30 Mr. Mark Gormley
  Why Approval Plans Fail

9:30- 10:30 Dr. H. William Axford
  Economics of Approval Plans

10:30- 11:00 Coffee Break

11:00- 12:30 Dealers' Panel:

Book Sellers Look at the Effect of Approval Plans: Their Point of View
Moderator: Mr. Hugh C. Atkinson

PANEL MEMBERS:

Mr. B. Dean Spain	Mr. Tom Martin
Mr. Jack Walsdorf	Mr. Nelson Bennion
Dr. Knut Dorn	Mr. Alexander Broude
Mr. Ralph Lessing	

P.M.

12:30- 2:00 Luncheon

 2:00- 3:00 Mr. Daniel Gore
     Adopting An Approval Plan for a College Library: The Macalester College Experience

 3:00- 3:15 Break

 3:15- 4:45 Approval Plan Workshop in Sections
     Participant has opportunity of attending two sections. Content will be repeated.

WORKSHOP IN SECTIONS a THROUGH g

    a. Mr. James L. Thompson
    b. Mr. Jack Walsdorf
    c. Dr. Knut Dorn
    d. Mr. Tom Martin
    e. Mr. Nelson Bennion
    f. Mr. Alexander Broude
    g. Mr. Ralph Lessing

Workshop will be repeated at 4:45 P.M.

7:30 - 9:00 Dealers by Appointment

FRIDAY, FEBRUARY 19, 1971

A.M.
 8:30- 9:00 Coffee

9:00- 10:00 Dr. LeMoyne W. Anderson
     Review of Efficient Internal Systems for Handling Approval Plans in Technical Services
10:00- 11:00 Miss Harriet K. Rebuldela
     Review of Approval Plan Methods
11:15- 11:30 Dr. Richard Chapin
     Summary Statement
11:30 Luncheon

ABOUT THE SPEAKERS & PANELISTS . . .

Dr. Lemoyne W. Anderson is Director of Libraries, Colorado State University.

Mr. Hugh C. Atkinson is Director of Libraries, Ohio State University.

Dr. H. William Axford is Director of Libraries, Arizona State University.

Mr. Nelson Bennion is Sales Manager, Bro-Dart.

Mr. Alexander Broude is President, Alexander Broude, Inc.

Dr. Richard Chapin is Director of Libraries, Michigan State University.

Dr. Knut Dorn is Head of Export Division, Otto Harrassowitz.

Mr. Daniel Gore is Director of Libraries, Macalester College.

Mr. Mark Gormley is Director of Libraries, Wayne State University.

Mr. David O. Lane is Chief Librarian, Hunter College, City University of New York.

Mr. Ralph Lessing is Vice President, Stechert-Hafner, Inc.

Mr. Tom Martin is Vice President, Richard Abel & Co.

Miss Harriet K. Rebuldela is Head of Bibliographic Searching Unit, University of Colorado

Mr. B. Dean Spain is Chairman of the Board, Baker & Taylor Co.

Mr. Peter Spyers-Duran is Director of Libraries, Florida Atlantic University.

Mr. James L. Thompson is Director of Marketing and Sales, Baker & Taylor Co.

Mr. Jack Walsdorf is Libraries Service Adviser, Blackwell's.

HOSPITALITY COMMITTEE
(Florida Atlantic University Library)

Marie Angelotti	Gloria Dahlberg	Elaine Kelly
Jill Beavers	Paul Donovan	Stephen Kerr
Rene Cardenas	Judy Ganson	Agatha Lyons
Phyllis Cartwright	Jeanne Henning	Lucy Parsons
Monroe Causley	Bruce Hurlbert	Margaret Stone

Grateful acknowledgment is here made for special assistance with hospitality arrangements, provided by the following firms:

Richard Abel & Company	Blackwell's
The Baker & Taylor Company	Bro-Dart Industries

Alexander Broude, Inc.
Otto Harrassowitz

BOARD MEMBERS

Dr. LeMoyne W. Anderson	Dr. Knut Dorn
Mr. Arthur Brody	Mr. Daniel Gore
Mr. Robert Davis	Mr. Mark M. Gormley

Mr. Tom Martin
Mr. B. Dean Spain
Mr. Peter Spyers-Duran

SEMINAR PLANNING

School Service Center
Mr. R. J. Kizlik

Appendix 2

The Participants

Anderson, LeMoyne W.—Colorado State University, Boulder, Colorado rado

Angelotti, Marie—Florida Atlantic University, Boca Raton, Florida

Atkinson, Hugh C.—Ohio State University, Columbus, Ohio

Axford, H. William—Arizona State University, Tempe, Arizona

Barksdale, Milton K.—Eastern Kentucky University, Richmond, Kentucky

Barron, R. Neil—Baker and Taylor Co., Somerville, New Jersey

Beavers, Jill—Florida Atlantic University, Boca Raton, Florida

Bennion, Nelson—Bro-Dart Industries, Williamsport, Pennsylvania

Birkhimer, R. E.—Southern Illinois University, Carbondale, Illinois

Bishop, Martha C.—University of Western Ontario, London, Ontario, Canada

Branch, Olive H.—University of Tennessee, Knoxville, Tennessee

Brody, Arthur—Bro-Dart Industries, Williamsport, Pennsylvania

Broude, Alexander—Alexander Broude, Inc., New York, New York

Bruhwiler, Annette B.—Fairleigh Dickinson University, Teaneck, New Jersey

Burkels, Mr. and Mrs. Leo—Swets & Zeitlinger, Berwyn, Pennsylvania

Caine, Beatrice—Georgia Institute of Technology, Atlanta, Georgia

Cameron, Jim—Richard Abel & Co., Inc., Portland, Oregon

Cardenas, Rene—Florida Atlantic University, Boca Raton, Florida

Cartwright, Phyllis B.—Florida Atlantic University, Boca Raton, Florida
Causley, Monroe S.—Florida Atlantic University, Boca Raton, Florida
Cecere, Charles—Kraus Periodicals Co., New York, New York
Chapin, Richard—Michigan State University, East Lansing, Michigan
Dahlberg, Gloria—Florida Atlantic University, Boca Raton, Florida
DeVolder, Arthur L.—University of New Mexico, Albuquerque, New Mexico
Donovan, Paul—Florida Atlantic University, Boca Raton, Florida
Dorn, Knut—Otto Harrassowitz, Wiesbaden, Germany
Dudley, Laura E.—Hofstra University, Hempstead, New York
Engel, A. Ferdinand—Western Kentucky University, Bowling Green, Kentucky
Farkas, Andrew—University of North Florida, Jacksonville, Florida
Franklin, Walter D.—Alfred University, Alfred, New York
Ganson, Judy—Florida Atlantic University, Boca Raton, Florida
Gardner, William M.—University of Kentucky, Lexington, Kentucky
Gilstrap, Max M.—University of Georgia, Athens, Georgia
Glaser, Edna—Four Continent Book Corp., New York, New York
Gore, Daniel—Macalester College, St. Paul, Minnesota
Gormley, Mark—Wayne State University, Detroit, Michigan
Griffin, Barry James—Alverno College, Milwaukee, Wisconsin
Hanes, Fred W.—Indiana State University, Terre Haute, Indiana
Hard, L. R.—McGill University, Montreal, Canada
Harwell, Richard—Georgia Southern College, Statesboro, Georgia
Heard, Joseph Norman—University of Southwestern Louisiana, Lafayette, Louisiana
Heidler, Louise W.—Miami University, Hamilton, Ohio
Heishman, Eleanor L.—Cornell University, Ithaca, New York
Henning, Jeanne—Florida Atlantic University, Boca Raton, Florida
Hilyard, Steven—New England College, Henniker, New Hampshire
Huang, Theodore S.—Fairleigh Dickinson University, Teaneck, New Jersey
Hughes, Charles Z.—University of Illinois, Chicago, Illinois
Hurlbert, Bruce—Florida Atlantic University, Boca Raton, Florida
Jabson, Betty S.—West Georgia College, Carrollton, Georgia
Jackson, W. Carl—Pennsylvania State University, University Park, Pennsylvania
Jans, Lucille—University of North Florida, Jacksonville, Florida

Jensen, Kenneth O.—University of Virginia, Charlottesville, Virginia
Kamens, Harry H.—University of Delaware, Newark, Delaware
Kelly, Elaine—Florida Atlantic University, Boca Raton, Florida
Kerr, Stephen—Florida Atlantic University, Boca Raton, Florida
Landis, Lois D.—Dickinson College, Carlisle, Pennsylvania
Lane, David O.—Hunter College, New York, New York
Lang, Sister Franz—Barry College, Miami, Florida
Lessing, Ralph—Stechert-Hafner, Inc., New York, New York
Lonnberg, Charles Mitchell—Indiana State University, Bloomington, Indiana
Lyons, Agatha—Florida Atlantic University, Boca Raton, Florida
Lyons, Sister Rita Claire—Saint Mary's College, Notre Dame, Indiana
Martin, Tom—Richard Abel & Co., Inc., Blackwood, New Jersey
Mason, Harold J.—Greenwood Press, Inc., Westport, Connecticut
McCabe, Gerard B.—Virginia Commonwealth University, Richmond, Virginia
McCleary, Douglas—Alexander Broude, Inc., New York, New York
McKann, Michael R.—University of Florida, Gainesville, Florida
Mellon, Priscilla E.—Florida Technological University, Orlando, Florida
Middlemiss, Robert W.—B. H. Blackwell, New Berlin, Wisconsin
Mitchell, Charity—University of Cincinnati, Cincinnati, Ohio
Mueller, Twyla—Eastern Michigan University, Ypsilanti, Michigan
Partenza, Myrna R.—Palm Beach Atlantic College, Palm Beach, Florida
Paulson, Merle J.—Wichita State University, Wichita, Kansas
Peeler, Elizabeth H.—University of West Florida, Pensacola, Florida
Randall, F. S.—Southern Illinois University, Carbondale, Illinois
Rebuldela, Harriet K.—University of Colorado, Boulder, Colorado
Ritti, Marie F.—Barry College, Miami, Florida
Roth, Harold L.—Nassau County Reference Library, Long Island, New York
Rouse, Roscoe—Oklahoma State University, Stillwater, Oklahoma
Rude, Darold—Indiana State University, Terre Haute, Indiana
Rundle, Allen G.—Baker and Taylor Co., Somerville, New Jersey
Schleifer, Harold B.—City University of New York, Bronx, New York
Spain, B. Dean—Baker and Taylor Co., Somerville, New Jersey
Spyers-Duran, Peter—Florida Atlantic University, Boca Raton, Florida
Stewart, Robert C.—University of Pennsylvania, Philadelphia, Pennsylvania

Stone, Margaret—Florida Atlantic University, Boca Raton, Florida
Talkington, Donald—Florida Atlantic University, Dade Center, Miami Beach, Florida
Thompson, James L.—Baker and Taylor Co., Somerville, New Jersey
Thompson, Leroy—Florida Memorial College, St. Augustine, Florida
Tongate, John T.—Sangamon State University, Springfield, Illinois
Tune, Ernest W.—School of Theology, Claremont, California
Waddlington, Ron—Richard Abel & Co., Inc., Atlanta, Georgia
Walsdorf, Jack—Blackwell's, New Britain, Wisconsin
Williams, Mary E.—Roosevelt University, Chicago, Illinois
Woodward, Rupert C.—George Washington University, Washington, D.C.
Yoast, Regina M.—Armstrong State College, Savannah, Georgia

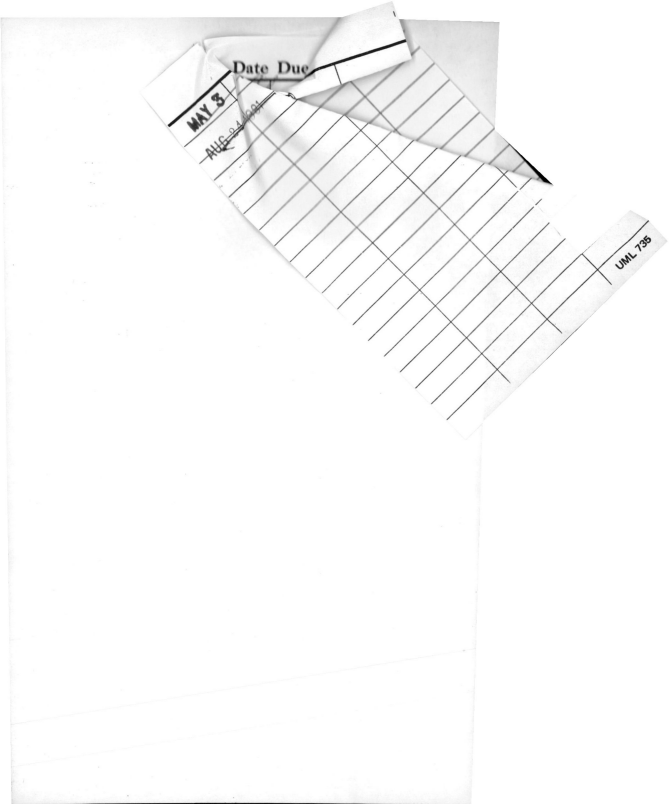